Published in 2018 by:
Helion & Company Limited
26 Willow Road
Solihull
West Midlands
B91 1UE
England
Tel. 0121 705 3393
Fax 0121 711 4075
email: info@helion.co.uk
website: www.helion.co.uk
Twitter: @helionbooks
Visit our blog http://blog.helion.co.uk/

Designed & typeset by Farr out Publications, Wokingham, Berkshire
Cover design by Farr out Publications, Wokingham, Berkshire
Printed by Henry Ling Limited, Dorchester, Dorset

ISBN 978-1-912390-34-2

British Library Cataloguing-in-Publication Data
A catalogue record for this book is available from the British Library

Cover:

CONTENTS

Note: In order to simplify the use of this book, all names, locations and geographic designations are as provided in *The Times World Atlas*, or other traditionally accepted major sources of reference, as of the time of the events described. For reasons of simplicity, genuine designations for Soviet/Russian-made weapons used in this book are mentioned once, and then their ASCC (or 'NATO') codes are used instead.

ABBREVIATIONS

AB	Air Base
AK	Russian for Automat Kalashnikova; general designation for a class of Soviet, or former East Block, manufactured 7.62mm assault rifles
APC	Armoured Personal Carrier
CAS	Close Air Support
COIN	Counterinsurgency
EROS	Eelam Revolutionary Organisation
IAP	International Airport
KIA	Killed in Action
Km	Kilometre
LTTE	Liberation Tigers of Tamil Eelam
MANPAD(S)	Man-portable air defence system(s) – light surface-to-air missile system that can be carried and deployed in combat by a single soldier
MiG	Mikoyan I Gurevich (the design bureau led by Artyom Ivanovich Mikoyan and Mikhail Iosifovich Gurevich, also known as OKB-155 or MMZ "Zenit")
PLOTE	People's Liberation Organization of Tamil Eelam
POW	Prisoner of War
Sqn	Squadron
SLA	Sri Lanka Army
SLAF	Sri Lanka Air Force
SLN	Sri Lanka Navy
STF	Special Task Force, the Sri Lanka Police dedicated counterinsurgency unit
TELO	Tamil Eelam Liberation Organisation
WIA	Wounded In Action

INTRODUCTION

This is the first volume in a mini-series covering the history of several inter-related military conflicts on Sir Lanka, which raged from 1971 until 2009. The wars in question not only shattered the fundamentals of the entire local society, but gradually developed into a massive conventional conflict that included the deployment of division-sized ground forces, and air and naval warfare of an intensity comparable with that of the Indo-Pakistani War of 1971.

As usual in the case of works of this kind, our research is based on a wide range of sources, including numerous scientific studies, official publications, as well as first-hand testimonies. As so often in the case of a relatively recent conflict, some of the perceptions in question are fiercely disputed. From the standpoint of both authors, this is little surprise: through our research and travels, the authors are uncomfortably familiar with many bloody wars fought in the so-called 'Third World' over the last 50 years, and the war on Sri Lanka is no exception from this rule. We consider any source to be relevant until it can be proven as without merit beyond any doubt. It is a matter of fact that governments, national and private organisations, private companies and certain individuals face harsh ramifications when their influence and/or participation in such conflicts become public. The authors therefore carefully collected all the available information, cross-examined various sources, corrected and updated their findings with the aim of offering the most detailed and dependable insight possible, with the objective of providing a comprehensive set of answers to questions like who, when, where, how and why.

While the emphasis of the coverage provided in these volumes is on military history, warfare never happens in a vacuum, but as a part of a wider context. Therefore, descriptions of geo-political circumstances are added as necessary. Although these are kept to an absolute minimum and used solely to explain the backgrounds for specific developments, the reader should be forewarned that this account is no attempt to provide a 'full spectrum' history of the Sri Lankan civil wars. Indeed, we have gone to great lengths in order to 'depoliticise' the narrative. This meant avoiding the use of terms such as 'regime', 'rebels', 'terror' or 'terrorist'. Clearly, one man's 'freedom fighter' is another's 'terrorist'. This book does not aim to judge the politics. Having no political axe to grind, the authors instead concentrated on recording and describing the military history of Sri Lanka, and have thus made all efforts to maintain a non-partisan narrative that remains readable and easy to understand.

CHAPTER I
THE ROOTS OF THE CONFLICT

The Island of Sri Lanka has been inhabited for at least 75,000 years. Its inhabitants were using iron tools, and cultivated fields from the 9th Century BC. About 400 years later, different tribes speaking Indo-Aryan languages began to settle on the island, mixed with domestic population and began coalescing into a single political entity – the Anuradhapura Kingdom, named after the city of the same name (founded in the 3rd Century BC). The Kingdom's population became known as the Sinhalese, after the name of one the tribes. Buddhism spread swiftly while the Anuradhapura kingdom grew ever more powerful and extended its control over virtually the entire island. During the subsequent centuries, dense trade links with South and South-Eastern Asia were developed, very large monasteries were built, and a gigantic and highly complex network of irrigation channels and cisterns came into being to sustain the Kingdom's increasing population. In the meantime, while Buddhism gradually lost influence in India and was superseded by a Hindu resurgence, Anuradhapura remained an essentially Buddhist kingdom, and this became one of its characteristics for the next few centuries, contrary to other parts of

A Portuguese illustration, showing Sinhalese women and children, at the time Westerners first reached the island they named Ceylon during the first half of the 16th Century. (Wikimedia Commons)

South-East Asia where the Hindu religion continued to spread.

The spread of Buddhism on Sri Lanka shows that the island kingdom was never an isolated entity. On the contrary, it was very much a part of the Indian subcontinent, whose evolutions, since the early ages, often had important repercussions of a cultural, religious, economic, but also political and military nature. Indeed, the Kingdom of Anuradhapura found itself at war with such powerful south-Indian Hindu Dravidian states such as the Pandyan, Pallava, or Cholas. By the 10th Century, Anudharapara had been weakened by internal rivalries and fell to a Cholan invasion. Although the Cholans were forced out by King Vijayabahu, in 1070, the capital of the kingdom was abandoned in favour of Polonnaruwa, which proved easier to defend.

Repeated invasions brought in their wake a significant Tamil population which added to Tamils that had settled on Sri Lanka since at least the 3rd Century BC. This presence in turn caused early conflicts – most of which should not be oversimplified or misunderstood as fought purely along Singhalese-Tamil lines, or even Hindu-Buddhist religious systems. On the contrary: Singhalese kings often used the services of Tamil mercenaries, while Anudharapara intervened several times on the Indian sub-continent too, and maintained alliances with local Tamil kingdoms. Indeed, the aforementioned Cholan invasion was largely the result of Anudharapara's alliance with the Pandyan Kingdom – which was another Tamil state. Similarly, south Indian invasions were often supported by factions within the Sinhalese Nobility that sought to seize the throne.

Unsurprisingly, successive waves of Tamil migrants from south India continued to settle on Sri Lanka, forming communities in the north and, to a lesser extent, south, interspersed with those of the Sinhalese, and progressively dominated by the Tamil. By the early 14th Century, the Jaffna Kingdom had emerged in northern Sri Lanka, ruled by a Tamil dynasty.[1]

In the period 1232-1396, Sri Lanka went through a period of recurrent instability, during which the Sinhalese state – although increasingly centralised – was gradually weakened, while successive Kings moved their capitals further south-west. This process ended with the foundation of Kotte, in 1396.[2] The Sinhalese state went through a brief period of resurgence during the reign of King Parakramabahu VI (1412-1467). Parakramabahu IV not only repulsed an invasion from the south Indian Vijayanagara Empire before conquering the Jaffna Kingdom in 1450 – with the help of an army including Tamil mercenaries – but also established political control of the whole island for the last time.[3] The situation began to unravel soon after his death: the Jaffna Kingdom was resurrected, while the Kotte Kingdom gradually lost power to the Kandy Kingdom. Correspondingly, by the early 16th Century, Sri Lanka was divided between the Tamil Jaffna Kingdom (with around 150,000 inhabitants), and the Sinhalese Kotte and Kandy Kingdoms (with about 400,000 inhabitants between them).[4]

The Portuguese, the Dutch and the British

While Sri Lanka maintained commercial links with China, Persian and various Arab nations for centuries, its first direct links with Europeans were established only in the early 16th Century. In 1515, a small Portuguese fleet dropped its anchors off Colombo. King of Kotte allowed the Portuguese to establish a fort and a trading post in the same area. Before long, the Portuguese began their efforts to dominate the island – greatly supported by the split of the Kingdom of Kotte into three parts. Although suffering severe defeats at the hands of one of resulting statelets, the Portuguese dominated the territories of the former Kotte Kingdom over the next 100 years. Furthermore, they established dominance over the Jaffna Kingdom, and annexed the same in 1619. To secure their grip upon Sri Lanka, the Portuguese constructed a series of coastal forts in locations like Galle, Mannar and Jaffna, while Catholic missionaries became active in converting the population to Christendom. However, the Portuguese never succeeded into establish their dominance over the Kandy Kingdom, whose armies managed to repeal several invasion attempts.

Meanwhile, the Portuguese began facing a new competitor: the Dutch. The latter were already influential in much of south-east Asia and dispatched several embassies to Kandy, between 1602 and 1638, resulting in an alliance against the Portuguese. Gradually, the latter were expelled from all of their possessions: Colombo fell to the Dutch in May 1656, Mannar in February 1658, and Jaffna in June of the same year. Thus ended the Portuguese presence on Sri Lanka, leaving the Dutch and the Kandy Kingdom as the only political powers. A new war soon erupted between the two former allies. The situation was settled by the division of responsibilities: the Dutch were left in the control of the coasts, while the Kingdom of Kandy controlled the inland.

The fall of The Netherlands to the French triggered an invasion of Sri Lanka by Great Britain. The isolated Dutch garrisons proved unable to offer any serious resistance and surrendered in 1796. Once they established themselves in control of the coast, and incorporated the island into the British Empire as the Crown Colony of Ceylon in 1802, the British concluded that an independent kingdom controlling the inland would be detrimental to their interests. Correspondingly, they invaded the Kandy Kingdom in 1803. Two columns of 2,000 troops each, supported by artillery, advanced from Colombo and Trincomalee, but both were repulsed. Learning their lesson, the British decided to capitalise upon never-ending rivalries that were plaguing Kandy's court: instead, they subdued the weakened kingdom through political and military action in 1815.

Two years later, a large uprising against the British rule erupted and quickly spread over most of Sri Lanka. Although suffering over 1,000 casualties – one fifth of the deployed force – the British gradually re-established their control in the course of the following counter-insurgency (COIN) campaign, which lasted until late 1818. In contrast, an insurrection of 1848 was swiftly crushed.[5] Ceylon was to remain firmly under British control for more than the next 100 years.

Sinhalese at War

Before the fall of Kandy, Sinhalese royals had managed to repeatedly defeat Western forces for nearly three centuries. Such a feat would not have been possible without the necessary know-how, based on experiences from earlier times. Indeed, the Sinhalese had rich military traditions, which were a result of various local factors as much as of their social organisation. With only about 600,000 inhabitants as of the early 16th Century, the island was relatively sparsely populated. Therefore, manpower was a precious resource and royal administrations carefully maintained a register of their subjects. Kandyan kings usually maintained a small standing army, whose mainstay was the Royal Guard – the Atapattu – and several specialised detachments. Between the 16th and 18th Century, the latter included the Vedikkara (cannoniers), the Vadana Tuvakku (musketeers), the Dunkara (archers), and the Vedibet Maduva (manufacturers of gunpowder). Support services included military music. Last, but not least, the permanent force included contingents of mercenaries – mostly of south Indian origin – paid directly by the Crown. Nevertheless, this army was always comparatively small: it

A Portuguese illustration of Sinhalese warriors, drawn around 1540. (Wikimedia Commons)

Vimaladharmasuriya I receiving Joris van Spilbergen, in 1603. (Wikimedia Commons)

Naval battle between the Dutch and Portuguese fleets, off Goa, in 1638. (Johannes Vigboons)

never exceeded more than a few thousand trained fighters when fully mobilised.

This permanent force formed a core around which additional forces were assembled as necessary. As the Crown owned all the land; correspondingly farming communities had to fulfil specific duties in exchange for their right to exploit the land. In Sri Lanka at that time, there were three main categories of rural settlements:

- Devalgam: villages supporting specific temples;
- Nindagam: villages supporting specific individuals; and
- Gabadagam: villages supporting the royal family.

In the latter case, one specific service requested from farmers was to provide one military-trained man per family when requested by the Crown. Ironically, when the Portuguese took over the Kotte Kingdom, they kept this system in place, and mobilized thousands of auxiliaries that way, which they called *lascarins*. Hence, the vast majority of the soldiers deployed by the Portuguese against the Sinhalese Kingdom of Kandy were Sinhalese, too.

The Kandyan royals regularly mobilized untrained peasants, although these were foremost used for logistical purposes. Their armies did not include any cavalry and the few horses were used as personal mounts of high-ranking officers. Elephants were used in battle, but also – and more importantly – for logistical purposes: their ability to carry heavy loads on rough terrain was unmatched and of particular importance in a country lacking roads. The resulting Sinhalese armies were foremost light infantry forces.

Their most common weapons were spears, spikes, swords and axes. The Sinhalese warriors only rarely wore any kind of armour, except for small shields. Javelins and composite bows (long and short) were in widespread use. Gunpowder appeared on Sri Lanka even before the arrival of the Portuguese, but muskets and harquebuses remained rare. Nevertheless, only a few decades later, firearms of high quality became common. The essence of their design was not a mere copy of Western weapons: most had longer barrels to increase the bullet velocity. Furthermore, the Kandyan made widespread use of the Gingals: light and small cannons firing projectiles weighting between four and twelve ounces, which proved better suited to the local geography (which made the movement of conventional, heavy artillery nearly impossible).[6]

Indeed, the geography of Sri Lanka was one of keys to the success of the Kandyan military. Because the heart of that kingdom was situated in the central, mountainous region, it was easy to defend. Any axes of advance – such like the Balana Pass – were easily predictable and thus defensible.

While terrain was the key, it was not the only reason: at least as important were new military practices developed by the Sinhalese since the Portuguese arrival. In 1521, only a few years after the establishment of first colonial settlements, the Kingdom of Kotte spit into Kotte, Sitavaka, and Raigama, ruled by the three sons of King Vijayabahu. Raigama was absorbed by Sitavaka in 1538, while the remaining two kingdoms became fierce rivals. The Kingdom of Kotte subsequently entered an alliance with the Portuguese, while the Sitavaka armies were reinforced by detachments of warriors deployed by the south Calicut Kingdom in southern India. During following wars between the Kotte-Portuguese coalition and Sitavaka, King Mayudunne and his son Rajasinhe proved to be gifted commanders.[7] They inflicted a major defeat upon the Kotte-Portuguese at Mulleriyawa, in 1562, and then took the city of Kotte, in 1565, after a very long siege. However, the Sitavaka armies failed to secure Colombo during two long sieges. This enabled Rajasinhe, King of Sitavaka, to defeat the Kotte-Portuguese coalition and then invade the Kingdom of Kandy (which remained neutral during the conflict between the Kotte-Portuguese and the Sitavaka), in 1582.

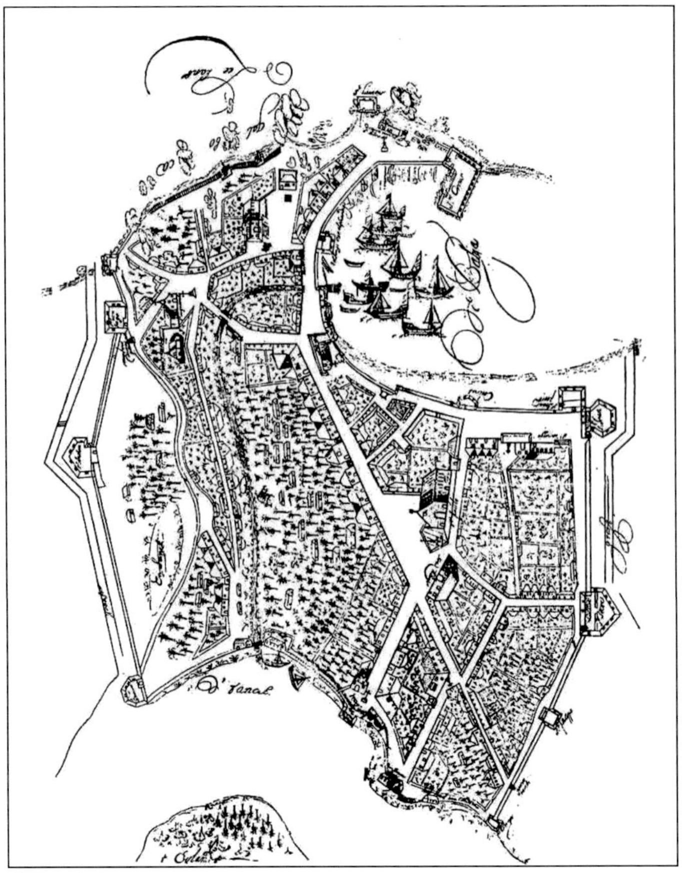

Plan view of Portuguese Colombo, from 1650. (Wikimedia Commons)

Two years later, the Portuguese launched their own campaign on Kandy, with the intention of placing their proxy on its throne. This enterprise proved successful, but the sovereign picked by the Portuguese died soon afterwards, and the thrown was taken over by Don Joao of Austria – a Sinhalese nobleman who had converted to Christianity and was in command of the local detachment of lascarins. Don Joao inaugurated his reign by re-converting to Buddhism, taking the name Vimaladharmasuriya, and expelling the Portuguese. Furthermore, he repulsed another invasion by Rajasinhe. With the latter dying soon after, the once mighty Sitavaka Kingdom unravelled swiftly and was absorbed by the Kotte Kingdom, which in turn was completely subjected to the Portuguese in 1580. The resulting situation was one where the Kandy and the Portuguese were the only major powers left on the Island.

In 1594, Captain-General Pedro Lopes de Souza invaded Kandy at the head of an estimated 1,000 Portuguese soldiers and 3,000 lascarins. His intention was to topple Vimaladharmasuriya and replace him with Dona Katarina – a converted Sinhalese noblewoman from the former Kandyan royal line, who would them marry a senior Portuguese officer and thus ensure the colonial domination. Because of his former cooperation with the Portuguese, Vimaladharmasuriya knew the strengths and weaknesses of the Westerners. Correspondingly, he devised a new strategy which was to be followed by successive Kandyan kings during the subsequent centuries: he did not oppose the Portuguese advance, but left the enemy progress ever deeper into his kingdom – even to occupy his capital. Then he cut their supply lines, forcing the Portuguese to live from the land. In order to collect food and supplies, the Portuguese were forced to deploy small detachments to the countryside, which in turn were repeatedly ambushed or harassed. Furthermore, the King managed to manipulate the Portuguese into executing the Sinhalese commander of their lascarins

Sri Rajadhi Rajasinhe, King of Kandy 1782-1798, on his throne. (Sketch by Jan Brandes)

contingent. As result, thousands of the Sinhalese warriors changed side and rallied their Kandyan counterparts. The rest of the invasion force had no other choice but to begin to retreat toward Colombo. It was only during this withdrawal, at the moment of highest Portuguese vulnerability, that Vimaladhasuriya committed the bulk of his army for a major showdown. In the course of several-days-long, running battle, he separated the Portuguese column into several parts and then annihilated these in separate actions. Only 93 Portuguese survived – and these were taken prisoners. Last, but not least, Dona Katarina was taken captive too: Vimaladharmasuriya married her soon after, thus legitimising his own dynasty.

This strategy of avoiding a large-scale battle with Western militaries; luring the enemy to penetrate deep into ill-suited terrain; severing supply-lines; using propaganda and deception to entice the lascarins to desert; and then attacking the enemy only once he was vulnerable, was repeated not only by Vimaladharmasuriya to defeat another Portuguese invasion in 1602, but also by Kings Senarath and Rajasinhe II, who repulsed similar attempts in 1630 and 1638. Even the first Dutch and British invasions of Kandy faced the same strategy.[8]

British Colonisation

The British rule over Ceylon resulted in far-reaching changes, the fundaments of which were provided by the Colebrooke-Cameron Commission in 1833. During the following decades, the island was re-organised into five provinces, and a rather limited representative system was created, at the top of which was a Legislative Council of 15, including three Ceylonese. Through the gradual expansion of the road system, and then several railway lines, different portions of the island became better connected than ever before. This was especially valid for the isolated central region, where large coffee plantations were created. A devastating leaf sickness of 1869 forced the landowners to replace coffee by tea. Subsequently, the local economy became export-oriented and resulted in the emergence of a local capitalist class, with all the associated institutions (like the Ceylon Bank, established in 1841). Furthermore, a small but efficient Civil Service was established. Schools were created with the aim of providing an educational system for the local people, and thus help create the necessary manpower. In 1931, the British imposed a new constitution, including universal suffrage.

By the time Ceylon was released into independence, in 1948, it was one of the richest countries in South Asia, capable of relying on an efficient public service, well-proven democratic institutions, and an excellently-trained – even if quantitatively limited – pool of administrators.[10]

However, some of such impressions were deceptive: colonial policies also left legacies that were soon to have far reaching consequences. Foremost, based on the classic 'divide and rule' politics, most British reforms favoured specific parts of the population while proving detrimental for everybody else. The result was that any Ceylonese who wanted to become a member of the local elites, had to be educated in Western-run schooling system. However, while perfectly sufficient for 1870s, when there were less than 20,000 students on the entire island, educational facilities remained limited in numbers and capacity, and their recruitment policies continued favouring wealthy locals, Christian Ceylonese, European expatriates, and so-called 'Burghers' (Ceylonese of mixed, sometimes Portuguese, Dutch or British backgrounds). Tamils were favoured too, especially by missionary schools, because churches were expecting the Hindu to be more amenable to convert, than Buddhists. About half of the first batch of students trained in the newly-established Colombo Medical Centre in 1872 were Tamils. By 1885, 300 out of 819 schools active on Ceylon were on the Jaffna Peninsula. Direct consequences of such practices were that by 1848, Christians and Burghers held 21% of the positions in the civil service, while Tamils held another 33%.

Meanwhile, one of the difficulties met by the British while adapting the central region to the cultivation of coffee, and latter tea, was the lack of a local population willing to work under extremely harsh

Martial Traditions of the Tamils

The military organisation of the Kingdom of Jaffna was similar to that of the Sinhalese. In that state, the military was the prerogative of the Marvar warrior cast. This was granted the right of living on the land provided by the king, who in turn had the right to call them to arms as necessary. Tamil warriors not only earned themselves an excellent reputation, and were often contracted as mercenaries by non-Tamil kings, but were taught martial values that included ritual suicide – for example to avoid dishonour or to demonstrate one's loyalty. Once the Jaffna Kingdom was conquered by the Portuguese, their culture gradually dissolved, and the Marvar were integrated into other castes. However, memories of their martial values survived in the classic Tamil literature and poetry. With the awakening of the Dravidian nationalism, remnants of such values were resurrected and were later to form the fundamentals of the LTTE's ideological fabric – in a similar fashion to the old Bushido martial code in Japan forming the fundamentals of the Imperial Japanese Army's ethos. For example, it is quite likely, that the 'Death instead of surrender' ethos of the LTTE was, at least indirectly, connected to the Marvar practices. Similarly, some of LTTE's publications at least reflected the concept of Moothinmullai: a warrior mother's duty to raise her children to die heroically in battle.[9]

'The Town of Colombo', illustration from a Dutch book from around 1775, based on original engraving by Johannes Kip, from 1680. (Wikimedia Commons)

An illustration of the Swiss Regiment de Meuron's which betrayed the Dutch and helped the British take over Ceylon. (Albert Escher painting, via wikicommons)

conditions. Correspondingly, ever larger number of Indian Tamils was 'imported' to Ceylon to satisfy demands for manpower from plantation owners. By 1911, around 500,000 Indian Tamils were recorded on the island, making up to 12% of the total population. Ironically, these new Tamil immigrants were never considered as equals by – and remained separated from – the original Tamil population.

Thus, the majority rural Sinhalese Buddhist population had reasons enough to feel antagonised and marginalised, even more so considering they were simultaneously submitted to continuously increasing taxation, necessary foremost to compensate for the losses suffered by the export economy when the latter went through a crisis in the mid-19th Century. Next, the colonial policies directly assaulted the very pillar around which Sinhalese rural life was organised: the Sangha – the Buddhist monk community. With the dissolution of the Kandyan monarchy, the British also dissolved the quasi-symbiotic relation between the state and the Sangha, resulting in massive losses of revenues and patronage for the latter. Land owned by, or devoted to the Sangha, was taken over by plantation owners, while Christian missionaries continued converting the population. Unsurprisingly, the monks began contesting Western influence. Their traditional status guaranteed that their opinions attracted numerous followers. Supported by activists that helped create new institutions in support of traditional religion, like Colonel Henry Steele Olcott, the Ceylonese Buddhism entered a phase of resurgence during the second half of the 19th Century and began actively campaigning against Christian missionaries.

Furthermore, some of charismatic monks – like Angarika Dharmapala – began to promote what could be defined as an 'early

A group of British-appointed Kandyan chiefs in the dress of traditional Dissawas, with Hon. J. P. Lewis, government agent, in 1905. (Wikimedia Commons)

Sinhalese nationalism'. This connected itself to the – distant but mighty – legendary Buddhist kingdoms of Anudharapara and Polonnaruwa, the ruins of which were re-discovered by archaeologists around the same time. Associating the Sinhalese 'race' with the Buddhism, and considering the Sinhalese the original and genuine inhabitants of the island, the first to develop a brilliant civilisation too, this nationalism soon developed strong antagonism against the Tamils. Henceforth, these were perceived not as local minority but as a part of a larger, Indian entity, and as traditional invaders. Suspicions among the Sinhalese nationalists were fuelled by the emergence of several minor movements in India of the early 20th Century, which advocated the creating of Dravidu Nadu – a Dravidian state that would have unified all the people identified as 'Dravidian', including the Tamils.

Overall, while frequently declared a 'colonial success story', Ceylon was marred by immense tensions that were boiling under the surface right from when the country was achieved independence. Indeed, it can be said that many seeds of the future civil war were sawn while Ceylon was still under the British rule.[11]

Official portrait of Honorary S. W. R. D. Bandaranaike, Prime Minister of Sri Lanka, who served from 1956 until his assassination in 1959. His widow played a crucial role in Sri Lankan politics over the following 20 years. (Wikimedia Commons)

Raising Tensions

The British released Ceylon into independence on 4 February 1948, and the country was then declared a 'Dominion within the British Commonwealth'. The local elites that inherited the rule from the British were divided into several political parties, including the United National Party (UNP) and the Sri Lanka Freedom Party (SLFP), representing most of the Sinhalese, the Tamil Congress (Ilangei Tamil Arasu, ITAK), and the Tamil State Party (also known as the Federal Party). With most of its members benefitting from the same, English-style, education the political class in charge of such movements was actually quite homogenous. Unsurprisingly, and despite the existence of some smaller formations of various ideologies, the UNP and the SLFP found it rather easy to dominate the political scene for the first few decades – even if always in fierce competition with each other. The UNP proved more successful early on: it ran the country immediately after its independence. The SLFP then created a coalition that won the elections of 1956 and 1970. Finally, the UNP recovered and won in 1977, starting a 17-year-long reign.

In the climate of competition between these two major Sinhalese parties, leveraging the widespread frustration caused by British policies proved a useful tool of attracting voters until (at least) the early 1970s. This helped reinforce a deleterious climate. Indeed, the gap between important segments of both the Sinhalese and the Tamil population widened ever more. Facing continuously increasing demands to 'correct' the unbalances generated by the British rule, the UNP and the SLFP gradually turned into prisoners of related ideologies: whenever their representatives attempted to find a compromise with the Tamils, they were immediately branded as 'traitors'.

The results of this situation were several de-facto 'anti-Tamil' laws. The first of these was adopted in 1949, when so-called 'Plantation Tamils' were deprived of their right to vote. Curiously, this bill was supported by several Tamil members of the parliament, who thus provided a clear illustration of the gap separating genuine, Ceylonese Tamil population, from 'British-imported' Tamil community of India. The next such act followed on 5 June 1956, when the SLFP-government adopted the 'Sinhala Only Act': this declared Sinhalese as the sole official language, and required fluency in this as mandatory for anybody trying to work in the civil services. Some of the Tamils reacted with protests: the same day, about 300 members of the Federal Party staged a demonstration in front of the parliament in Colombo. In revenge, extremist Sinhalese launched anti-Tamil riots. By the time the security services managed to restore order, about 150 – mostly Tamils – had been killed. Another series of anti-Tamil riots followed in May 1958. On 25 September 1959, an extremist monk assassinated Solomon West Ridgway Dias Bandaranaike. In February 1961, the Federal Party initiated a large wave of protests and civil disobedience against the government in Jaffna, Vavuniya, Batticaloa, Trincomalee, Mannar and Mullaitivu. The government reacted by imposing the state of emergency on 17 April 1961, and arrested several Tamil parliamentarians. Although lasting for nearly two years, protests failed to reverse pro-Sinhalese policies. On the contrary: the situation gradually calmed down and the state of emergency was lifted in 1963.

On 22 May 1972, the SLFP government led by Sirimavo Bandaranaike (Solomon's widow who rose to power following elections in 1970, and adopted a new, republican constitution), re-named the country into Sri Lanka, and assigned a pre-eminent status to Buddhism.[12] Next, Bandaranaike's government modified the rules for the admission to universities, with the goal of limiting the number of Tamils accessing higher education – where they had still been 'over-represented': henceforth, Tamil candidates (who still made up upto 35% of students admitted to science faculties) had to score higher marks than their Sinhalese counterparts. Bandaranaike's politics towards rural development envisaged new irrigation schemes for the dryer regions of Sri Lanka, and re-settlement of Sinhalese farmers to cultivate the same regions. However, most of these were already populated by a Tamil majority, which understood related activity as an attempt to modify the local demography. To add salt to the injury, Sri Lanka went through a period of economic crisis, felt strongly by all of its population. Amid raising tensions, the Tamil Congress, the Federal Party, and several other movements joined their efforts and formed the Tamil United Front. Re-named into the Tamil United Liberation Front (TULF) a few years later, the leaders of this movement announced their objective to create an independent country – the Tamil Eelam. Furthermore, a small segment of the Tamil youth had concluded that the traditional political parties were much too inept in defending the rights of their voters, and that the goal of Tamil Eelam could only be reached through armed action. These were the seeds for a civil war.[13]

CHAPTER 2
THE SRI LANKAN ARMED FORCES

The origins of the modern armed forces of Sri Lanka can traced back to the times of the British colonial rule. Although considering the local population as 'ill-adapted to military service', the British raised four Ceylonese regiments between 1802 and 1814. Three of these were disbanded between 1815 and 1820. However, the 1st Ceylon Regiment remained operational and was re-organized as the Ceylon Rifle Regiment in 1825, before being dissolved in 1874.

Seven years later a new unit, the Ceylon Light Infantry Volunteers, was established. This was staffed by 210 Europeans and 156 Ceylonese. Several minor components – all staffed by volunteer residents, and including a small artillery unit, a mounted infantry company (which took part in the Boer War, in South Africa), the Planters Rifle Corps, and the Medical Corps – were added during the following years. By 1910, these formed the centrepiece of the Ceylon Defence Force (CDF). For the next 38 years – i.e. until independence – the British considered the CDF an 'auxiliary force', unsuitable for anything else but second-line duties. Correspondingly, the Ceylonese were never deployed anywhere outside their country, although the Ceylon Light Infantry Volunteers gradually grew in strength to five battalions, and included coastal- and anti-aircraft artillery units, totalling about 15,000. When the threat of a Japanese invasion failed to materialise, in 1942, the CDF's involvement in World War II remained limited to its anti-aircraft crews firing at the aircraft of the Imperial Japanese Navy, when these raided the ports of Colombo and Trincomalee, on 5 and 9 April 1942, respectively.

Most of the CDF was de-mobilised in 1945. However, the result of related recruitment and training efforts was a build-up of a cadre of Ceylonese officers and non-commissioned officers (NCO), who gained significant experience. Indeed, they were to form the core around which a national army was to be built following independence.[14]

Guard of Honour by the Ceylon Army for Brigadier James Sinclair, Earl of Caithness, in 1950. (Wikimedia Commons)

Royal Ceylon Army

On 10 October 1949, the government of Ceylon ordered the establishment of the Royal Ceylon Army (RCA). This new institution integrated the former CDF and was originally intended to include both units staffed by regulars and volunteers (the latter to be activated only in the time of crisis). The RCA followed the British organisational practices and was based around the same regimental system. Initially, it was supported by a small number of British advisors, who helped

Training of the RCyAF Regiment in the Ground Combat and Recruit Training Unit in the jungle of Diyatalawa. Officers of the Royal Ceylonese Army underwent similar courses provided by the SAS in Borneo. (SLAF)

create all of the specialised units (including the Armoured, Field Artillery, and Engineers Regiments), and its first two commanders – Brigadier Roderick Sinclair (1949-1952) and Brigadier Francis Reid (1952-1955) – were both British. A Sinhalese officer, Major-General Anton Muttukumaru, took over only in 1955.

Each of the Infantry Regiments of the RCA included several battalions, but none was responsible for their operational deployment. Instead, battalions were assigned directly to the army headquarters – and, later on, to regional commands and brigade headquarters – whenever on operational deployment. Notable is that there were regular and volunteer battalions, that some of the latter were often permanently mobilised during the following war, and that their effectiveness and readiness regularly reached those of their regular counterparts. A notable exception was the National Guard Regiment, established in 1989, which included battalions of volunteers only.

The first regular infantry unit was the 1st Ceylon Light Infantry Battalion, established on 12 May 1950. This was followed (in chronological order of their establishment) by the 2nd (Volunteer) Ceylon Light Infantry Battalion, the 1st Coastal Artillery Regiment (responsible for the defence of the port of Trincomalee), the Anti-Aircraft Artillery Regiment, and the 2nd (Volunteer) Artillery Regiment. A third artillery unit – the 3rd Field Artillery Regiment – was activated in 1953, while two additional infantry regiments (the Ceylon Sinha Regiment and the Gemunu Watch Regiment) came into being in October 1959 and December 1962.[15] Standard practice for each of the regiments was to include two battalions: one regular, and another volunteer.

The RCA activated numerous support units during its first decade of existence, including the Service Corps, the Corps of Military Police (established in October 1949), the Corps of Ordnance and the Corps of Ceylon Electrical and Mechanical Engineers (established in December 1949 and in March 1950, respectively), the 1st Field Engineer Regiment (established in 1959), the 3rd Works Service Ceylon Engineers, and an Army Training Centre.

Another significant unit came into being on 10 October 1955, when the Reconnaissance Squadron was created. Including a core of 7 officers and 160 other ranks, this was initially equipped with six Ferret Mk. I and Mk. II scout cars, and BSA motorcycles and side-cars. Three years later, this unit was expanded into the Reconnaissance Regiment (including the A and B Squadrons, each of which consisted of three troops) and equipped with 12 Daimler armoured cars. The introduction of armoured vehicles proved an exception rather than the rule, because most of equipment dated back to the times of World War II. Indeed, successive governments saw no need to invest in the armed forces as there was no external threat. Therefore, funding of the army – which received less than 50% of the defence budget, itself mere 1-2% of the national budget – remained limited. It only increased as the governmental revenues increased, from US$ 2,541,707 in 1953 to 6,362,659 in 1960. A decade later, it reached US$ 7,607,428, which was an equivalent to only 1.10% of the national budget. Unsurprisingly, the total manpower remained essentially the same through this period: even as of 1970, there were only 6,620 regulars (including 329 officers) and 5,655 volunteers (including 67 officers).

It was only during and immediately after the insurrection of 1971,

Table 1: SLA's Major Combat Units, late 1970s

Unit	Establishment Date	Notes
1st Battalion Sri Lanka Light Infantry	1950	1st SLLI
2nd Volunteer Battalion Sri Lanka Light Infantry	1950	2nd (V) SLLI
1st Battalion Sir Lanka Sinha Regiment	1956	1st Sinha
2nd Volunteer Battalion Sri Lanka Sinha Regiment	1956	2nd (V) Sinha
3rd Volunteer Battalion Sir Lanka Sinha Regiment	1969	3rd (V) Sinha
1st Battalion Gemunu Watch Regiment	1962	1st GWR
2nd Volunteer Battalion Gemunu Watch Regiment	1964	2nd (V) GWR
3rd Volunteer Battalion Gemunu Watch Regiment	1965	3rd (V) GWR
1st Reconnaissance Regiment	1959	1st RR
1st Field Engineer Regiment	1959	1st FER
4th Field Regiment Sri Lanka Artillery	1962	76mm Mountain Guns, 85mm guns from China

that the RCA experienced a significant intake of new arms, including 85mm Type 56 guns from China. A year later, additional Ferret Mk. IIs and Saladin armoured cars were imported from Great Britain, and BTR-152 armoured personnel carriers (APCs) from the Union of Soviet Socialist Republics (USSR, also 'Soviet Union'), while the three services were re-designated as the Sri Lanka Army (SLA), the Sri Lanka Air Force (SLAF), and the Sri Lanka Navy (SLN). The new vehicles were used to double the size of the 1st Reconnaissance Regiment, which had four fully-equipped squadrons by 1974. However, introduction of BTR-152 did cause some problems – primarily related to the lack of technical documentation in the English language and Moscow refusing to deploy any advisors.

This diminutive army ran regular exercises, staged using the tactics of conventional warfare. Its first battalion-sized manoeuvre, 'Operation Tyro', took place in 1954. Starting in 1956, the RCA changed the emphasis to counter-insurgency (COIN) operations. Correspondingly, several NCOs were assigned to the British force in Malaya, where they received COIN training and training in jungle combat. Furthermore, two officers were trained in guerrilla warfare in Yugoslavia. Otherwise, training of the officer corps remained heavily influenced by the British: six cadets underwent training at the Sandhurst Academy in the 1950s, while during the following decade additional officers were trained in Australia, India and Pakistan. In order to save money, all training abroad was cancelled, starting in 1968, and cadets trained in-country only.[16]

The general situation of the SLA remained similar through the 1970s. Several thousands of SLR rifles enabled a wholesale re-equipment of infantry formations. Another batch of 12 Saladin and three Ferrets arrived in 1979. However, the total strength of the army remained de-facto much the same as previously, despite rising tensions in the north. By 1979, the SLA thus still counted only 9,125 regulars (including 496 officers); there were 8,495 volunteers, but only 109 of their 671 officers were actually mobilised. Organisation of major combat units was as provided in Table 1.[17]

From Royal Ceylon Navy to Sri Lanka Navy

The Ceylon Navy Act of 9 December 1950, marked the birth of the Royal Ceylon Navy (RCyN). Although a new service, this branch could rely on still fresh experience of the Ceylon Royal Navy Reserve, created by the British in 1937 that, on full mobilisation, included 926 officers and other ranks, and manned a miscellaneous fleet of minesweepers, tugs and other auxiliary vessels. Although demobilised after the end of World War II, 9 officers and 91 sailors were kept on active duty and these formed the core of the RCyN.

The navy's first ship, HMCyS *Viyaya*, was an Algerine-class minesweeper donated by Great Britain. In 1952, she was deployed to patrol the Palk Straits to combat illegal immigration and endemic smuggling, in the course of the Operation Weback, but proved ill-suited for this role (primarily because of shallow waters and plentiful lagoons that are characterising most of the island's northern coast). Correspondingly, in 1955, the navy acquired several patrol boats.

Meanwhile, significant efforts to recruit and train additional personnel were launched in 1955, when Commodore Del Mele took over as commander. As the first Ceylonese to command this branch, Del Mele launched a very ambitious expansion program. By 1958, he graduated 48 officers and 510 sailors, and acquired HMCyS *Parakrama* (another Algerine-class minesweeper), HMCyS *Mahasena* and HMCyS *Gajabahu* (two former Israeli River-class frigates). While the latter two had all of their anti-submarine warfare equipment removed, and armament reduced to three 4.7 inch guns, they proved to be a mixed blessing: *Gajabahu* constantly suffered from defective machinery, and spent much of her career with the RCyN undergoing repairs.

Eventually, Del Mele's 'Blue Sea' policy proved over-ambitious and too costly. During the 1960s, emphasis was placed on developing shore-control capabilities. Correspondingly, *Mahasena*, *Viyaya* and *Parakrama* had been withdrawn from service and sold for scrap, by 1965, while *Gajabahu* was relegated to training purposes. Instead, the RCyN acquired more than 20 Vosper-Thorneycroft patrol boats. Capable of reaching speeds in excess of 25 knots and equipped with search-lights, these small vessels were operating from the ports of Colombo and Trincomalee. Despite their intensive patrolling activity, the navy proved unable to curb the smuggling activity and the insurrection of the People's Liberation Front (Janatha Vimukthi Peramuna, JVP; see Chapter 3 for description). The situation was worsened by the lack of ground troops trained to operate in conjunction with warships and protect naval facilities. As a result, the navy was forced to mobilise and deploy many of its sailors – including the crew of *Gajabahu* – for security duties, while the government was forced to request Indian support in patrolling its coasts.

Such deficiencies were addressed only in 1972, when the SLN began to commission more powerful vessels. At first, two Type 062 fast gun boats – SLNS *Sooraya* and *Weeraya* – were acquired from China. These packed a comparatively heavy fire-power in form of two 37mm twin-cannons, and two 25mm twin-cannons. Although they proved not to be ideal for operations close to the coast, they came very cheap, because Beijing was ready to sell them 'at friendship prices'. Therefore, three additional vessels of this class – *Dakshaya*, *Ranakamee* and *Balawatha* – followed in 1973, and two others (*Jagatha* and *Rakshaka*) in 1980. Meanwhile, the Soviet Union donated a single Project 206 torpedo boat (*Samudra Devi*), in 1980, and five patrol craft (including *Seruwa* and *Korawakka*) were ordered in Great Britain.

When forced to replace worn-out Vosper-Thorneycroft patrol boats in 1976, the navy placed an order for four coastal patrol craft with the Colombo Dockyards. Well-satisfied, the SLN ordered additional batches of the same class in 1978 and 1980 again. Meanwhile, the frigate *Gajabahu* had been withdrawn from service in 1976.

Total manpower of the Sri Lanka Navy remained stabile through

The first helicopters in service with the RCyAF were two Westland S.Mk 51 Dragonflies. Shown is the example with the serial CH501. (Albert Grandolini Collection)

One of three Airspeed Oxfords obtained by the Royal Ceylonese Air Force in 1953. (Albert Grandolini Collection)

most of the 1960s and 1970s, at around 2,400.[18]

Royal Ceylon Air Force

The Royal Ceylon Air Force (RCyAF) came into being on 2 March 1951 – fully two years after the ratification of the Air Force Act, on 3 October 1949. Contrary to the army and the navy, this service had to start virtually from the scratch, because there were only four Ceylonese nationals with relevant experience from serving with the Royal Air Force (RAF) of Great Britain, at earlier times. Nevertheless, London was willing to provide necessary advice and support. Furthermore, the RCyAF inherited a relatively well-developed network of air bases constructed during World War II, and including Ratmalana, Katunayake (former Negambo), China Bay, Hingurakgoda (former Minneriya), Vavuniya, Palali (former Kankeesanhurai), Sigiriya, Koggala, Weerawila, and Puttalam. All were to provide invaluable services during following decades – although the RCyAF operated only from Katunayake during the first years of its existence.

On its establishment, the air force included four Ceylonese nationals, three officers (including its commander, Group-Captain Graham Clerke Bladon) and 20 NCOs seconded from the RAF. Its sole vehicles were two trucks – with appropriate registration plates: AF2001 and AF2002. Unsurprisingly, during its first decades, air force's emphasis was on recruitment and training of local personnel. The first Ceylonese cadets were trained at home before continuing their education in Great Britain. Subsequently, such practices proved unnecessary because the RCyAF proved perfectly able to train all its pilots and ground personnel at home: 840 officers and other ranks graduated in 1959 and 1,260 by 1962. Furthermore, and in full traditions of the RAF, the air force established its own Air Force Regiment, responsible for protection of ground bases, in 1956. The process of initial establishment and formation lasted until 1966, by when the air force was completely staffed by local personnel from top to bottom. The first Ceylonese commander of the air force was Commodore Ekanayake Roham Amarasekera, a veteran of the RAF's Bomber Command, appointed to this position in 1962.

The first RCyAF aircraft were four Chipmunk T.Mk 10 trainers, acquired in October 1950. These were followed by two additional batches – one of five, the other of three – Chipmunks, purchased in 1952 and 1953, and three Airspeed Oxford Mk Is. Twelve Boulton Paul Balliol T.Mk 2 trainers were delivered in 1954, followed by six de Havilland 104 Doves, four Prestwick Pioneer short-take-off and landing aircraft, and two Westland S.Mk 51 Dragonfly helicopters, in 1955.[19]

The influx of aircraft enabled the air force to divide its Flying Wing into two squadrons, numbered 1 and 2, on 1 September 1957: all the Chipmunks and Balliols were operated by the No. 1 Squadron, which served as a training unit, while all the Pioneers, Doves, Oxfords and Dragonflies served with No. 2 Squadron, which primarily served

One of little-known types operated by the RCyAF in the 1960s were four Prestwick Pioneer (Scottish Aviation Pioneer) short-take-off and landing aircraft, used for liaison and as light transports. (Albert Grandolini Collection)

For nearly 30 years, DHC-1 Chipmunk T.Mk 10s – the first aircraft of the RCyAF – served as basic trainers for generations of Sri Lankan pilots. (SLAF)

The DH.104 Dove, six of which were acquired in 1955, was one of most important light transports in service with the RCyAF and then the SLAAF of the 1960s and 1970s. (SLAF)

The Jet Provost was the first jet aircraft in service with the RCyAF: 12 were acquired in 1960. This pre-delivery photograph is showing underwing armament – consisting of up to eight bombs of 50lbs, and four unguided rockets – to advantage (BAE Heritage)

Between helicopters rushed to Sri Lanka in 1971, were six Bell 47Gs (or OH-13Hs) from surplus stocks of the US Army. Painted Olive Drab overall, they rarely wore any kind of markings. (Albert Grandolini Collection)

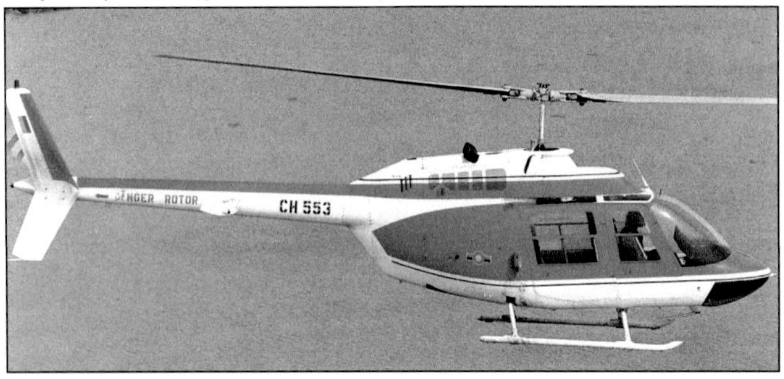

The first from the second batch of six additional Bell 206 Jet Rangers operated by the RCyAF and then the SLAF wore the serial CH-553. Used for VIP-transport and – during the insurgency of 1971 – for transporting supplies, but also as light strikers, all Bell 206s of the early 1970s wore 'civilian-style' livery in white and bright red. (Albert Grandolini Collection)

Sri Lanka received only one MiG-15UTI, but this provided valuable service in preparing pilots for MiG-17 operations. (Albert Grandolini Collection)

for transport purposes. Oxfords and Balliols were withdrawn from service in 1958 and 1959, respectively, and 12 Jet Provosts acquired instead. These were the first jets of the RCyAF, and the Ceylonese pilots converted to them without any problems – although one Jet Provost crashed in Negambo Lagoon, following an engine flame-out, in 1960. The pilot, Squadron Leader N. H. Lokuge, ejected safely.

Availability of Jet Provosts dramatically increased the firepower of the air force, and pilots thus began training for close-air support (CAS) operations. Furthermore, transport capabilities were increased through acquisition of four de Havilland 114 Herons, in 1959-1960, all of which were assigned to No. 2 Squadron.

Following quick and trouble-free development of the 1950s, the RCyAF experienced a decade of no further expansion: as the economy slowed down during the 1960s, not a single new aircraft or helicopter was purchased. On the contrary, although a Flight School had been established at China Bay in 1963, proving too costly, all the Jet Provosts were mothballed, remaining Pioneers and Dragonflies were withdrawn from service, and the only reinforcements for the air force were three Bell 206 Jet Rangers, acquired in 1968 and deployed by the No. 4 Helicopter Flight.[20]

Expansion of the SLAF in 1971-1972

The decade of stagnation ended abruptly in early April 1971, due to the JVP insurgency. In response to urgent requests from Colombo, the air force was literally flooded with new equipment of entirely different origin. On 22 April 1971, Antonov An-22 transports of the Soviet Air Force's Transport Aviation delivered five MiG-17s and one MiG-15UTI, a pair of Kamov Ka-26 helicopters, and several radar systems to Sri Lanka. By 1972, also six Bell 47Gs and six additional Jet Rangers were acquired from the USA, as were six Cessna 150s and 337s. This expansion resulted in the air force activating new squadrons and being re-organised as detailed in Table 2.

The quick build-up of 1971-1972 did not prove long-lasting. On the contrary, the SLAF was soon forced to realize that its budget remained limited. In an attempt to save money, the personnel of the air force refurbished two of the Herons in 1972, and replaced their Gypsy Queen Mk.30 engines with modern Lycoming IO540 – with some help from the Riley Turbostream Corporation (which provided the necessary blueprints). Furthermore, the SLAF established its commercial branch, named Helitours. The centrepiece of the same was a flight of Jet Ranger helicopters, used to fly tourists around the island, and for ferry-flights to the Maldives. The latter proved so successful that also a Convair 440 Metropolitan airliner was acquired, and in 1974 the SLAF was contracted to help set up the Air Maldives Company, which operated two Convairs.

Through the related work, personnel of the SLAF's Technical Maintenance Depot reached levels of skills enabling it to refurbish two worn-out Douglas DC-3s of Air Ceylon. They entered service with No. 2 Squadron in 1975, with registrations CR821 and CR822. Another former mount of Air Ceylon, an Avro HS.748, followed in 1978, by when the shortage of fuel and spares forced the air force to drastically reduce its activities. Correspondingly, No. 3 and No. 5 Squadrons were absorbed into No. 2 and No. 4 Squadrons, while No. 6 Squadron was disbanded without replacement. Furthermore, all the MiGs, Jet Provosts, and Ka-26s were withdrawn from service. Therefore, by the end of 1979, the SLAF was down to three operational squadrons[21]

Jack of all Trades, Master of None?

As an institution, the Ceylonese military was far from being isolated from the political turmoil that impacted society at large – even more

Table 2: Order of Battle of the SLAF, 1972-1979

Unit	Equipment	Base
No. 1 Flight Training School	Jet Provost, Cessna 150	China Bay
No. 2 Transport/Helicopter Squadron	Dove, Heron/Riley-Heron, Convair 440, HS.748	Katunayake
No. 3 Squadron	Cessna 337	China Bay, disbanded 1979
No. 4 Helicopter Squadron	Jet Ranger, Ka-26	Katunayake
No. 5 Squadron	Bell 47G	Katunayake, disbanded 1979
No. 6 Squadron	MiG-17, MiG-15UTI	Katunayake, disbanded 1979

RCyAF and SLAF Serial Number System

Originally all RCyAF aircraft wore registrations starting with the prefix C, standing for Ceylon. The next letter referred to the purpose of the aircraft or helicopter in question. These letters were followed with a number ranging from 101 to 999, sometimes issued randomly. This is why exact details of the numbers used on some of types remain unknown today.[22]

Table 3: RCyAF and SLAF Serials

Prefix	Meaning/Purpose
A	Attack
C	Communication
F	Fighter
FT	Fighter Trainer
H	Helicopter
J	Jet
R	Reconnaissance
T	Trainer
X	Experimental

Table 4: Known Serial numbers of RCyAF and SLAF Aircraft, 1951-1979

Type	Total Number	Serial
Balliol	12	CA301 – CA312
Oxford	3	CC203 (only known serial)
Pioneer	4	CC602, CC603, CC604
Cessna 337	Unknown	CC650, CC652, CC656, CC660
Dragonfly	2	CH501, CH502
MiG-15UTI	1	CF901
MiG-17F	5	CF903, CF904, CF905, CF906 (probable range was CF902 – CF906)
Ka-26	2	CH515, CH516
SA.365C	2	CH531, CH532
Bell 206A	9	CH550, CH553, CH554, CH556, CH557, CH558
Bell 212	6	CH561, CH562, CH563
Bell 47G/OH-13H	6	CH580
Jet Provost	12	CJ701, CJ702, CJ703, CJ704, CJ705, CJ706, CJ707, CJ708, CJ709, CJ710, CJ711, CJ712
Heron	4	CR801, CR802, CF803, CR804; CR803 & CR804 converted to Riley Heron
Convair 440	1	CR811
DC-3/C-47	2	CR821, CR822
HS.748	1	CR830
Dove	6	CS401, CS404, CS406
Chipmunk	12	CT101 – CT111
Cessna 150	Unknown	CT150, CT152, CT153

A front view a Sri Lankan Jet Provost, together with most of the armaments deployed by this type. The latter included unguided 78mm rockets, and 50lb (25kg) bombs. (SLAF)

so because its officer corps was strongly reflecting the British elite-building politics. Indeed, up to 60% of the officer corps was either Tamil, Burghers, or Christian Sinhalese, while the rank and file of the other ranks was closer to the ethnic composition of the Ceylonese population. During the second half of the 1950s, the government introduced measures to reinforce the recruitment of Buddhist Sinhalese – often in the face of fierce opposition from senior officers. Unsurprisingly, this resulted in some dissent between the rank and file. In January 1962, 16 officers of the army, navy, and the police were arrested and charged with plotting a coup d'état. Because eight of these were from the Artillery Corps, the 1st and 3rd Artillery Regiment were both disbanded on 25 April 1962, and reorganized as the 4th Artillery Regiment – manned by elements drawn from the two dissolved units but considered 'loyal'. Similarly, several support units were disbanded and replaced by new formations with identical functions. Subsequently, the scale of exercises was reduced to company-sized operations. Ironically, when another coup was – allegedly – plotted by several Sinhalese Buddhist NCOs, in 1965, the accused were acquitted: it turned out that they planned to topple the newly-elected UNP government out of the fear it might reverse the SLFP's politics.

Through all of this time, the armed forces of Ceylon and then Sri Lanka were heavily taxed with duties that severely impeded their training. Almost immediately upon its creation, the navy was mobilised to reinforce the Customs Department, while the air force was involved in anti-immigrant operations already as of 1953. Later on, Prestwick Pioneers were used for crop spraying, too. The army suffered the most from the situation, then while crop dusting allowed RCyAF's pilots to at least log some flight hours and train navigation and low-altitude flying, there was no replacement for the training of the ground forces.

In 1952, two companies of the 1st Ceylon Light Infantry were deployed to Mannar within Operation Monty, with the task of patrolling the coast and arresting illegal immigrants from south India. A year later, the Army was ordered to support the police in Colombo and man checkpoints during strikes caused by increasing prices of food. The army was mobilised again during the riots of 1958 and then deployed – together with the navy and air force – on Jaffna, during protesting in that area in 1962. Meanwhile, the army was requested to help the police in conducting regular law enforcement operations. In 1957, the 3rd Field Artillery Regiment was deployed to search and destroy so-called Ganja plantations. All through the 1960s and 1970s, different army units were repeatedly deployed for anti-immigration patrolling, while engineer troops were used in development works, and to clear land for cultivation. Indeed, by the late 1970s, the military was expected to help the police repress even highway robbers, prevent illicit timber cutting, and to provide training for the youth participating in the National Development Service. Unsurprisingly, an army report from 1978 concluded:

With the Sri Lankan police hopelessly overwhelmed by its own tasks, Army troops were frequently deployed for such mundane tasks as regulating traffic. (Albert Grandolini Collection)

> The state of preparedness of the Army for conventional operations is not satisfactory…it had also not been possible to carry out training in these tasks on account of the duties, which the Army had been called upon to perform.[23]

In an attempt to remedy the situation, in 1959 the Army established the Pioneer Corps: this 14,000 strong volunteer unit served as a labour force to take over the work the strikers refused to do. It saw its first action in 1961, when Pioneers were deployed to secure the port of Colombo when dock workers went on strike threatening to cause a major food crisis in the country. Obviously, this proved anything other than enough. Therefore, although possessing a significant core of well-trained and highly-competent officers and NCOs, with excellent know-how and strong set of traditions, the armed forces of Sri Lanka were ill-prepared for what happened already in 1971, not to talk about subsequent times. They were much too small, under-financed, and so severely distrusted by their political masters, that although constantly engaged in operations related to internal security, they hardly found the time to train for conventional, semi-conventional, or COIN operations. Nevertheless, the fundamentals were available and, with time, were to provide the armed forces with sound foundations for further expansion. Foremost, achievements gained during the first two decades of their existence, and strong traditions, enabled the Sri Lankan military to maintain cohesiveness despite often tremendous hardships – and not a few outright disasters – it went through.

CHAPTER 3
RISING INSURGENCIES

The first large-scale insurgency in the country did not erupt because of the growing Tamil-Sinhalese rift, but was the product of the emergence of a Sinhalese ultra-leftist movement, the JVP, which launched a full-scale insurrection in April 1971 and plunged the country into chaos.

Other than large movements like the UNP and the SLFP, the Ceylonese political scene included the Communist Party, founded in 1943. By the mid-1960s, this had split in two rival organisations with one maintaining allegiance to Moscow while the other was pro-Chinese. The pro-Beijing wing of the party split: a faction of dissenters led by Rohana Wijeweera, a young and charismatic activist who had studied medicine in the Soviet Union between 1960 and 1962, left the Party and created their own organization in 1967, the JVP.

This militant group structured itself along conventional Leninist patterns. It included a 25-member political committee

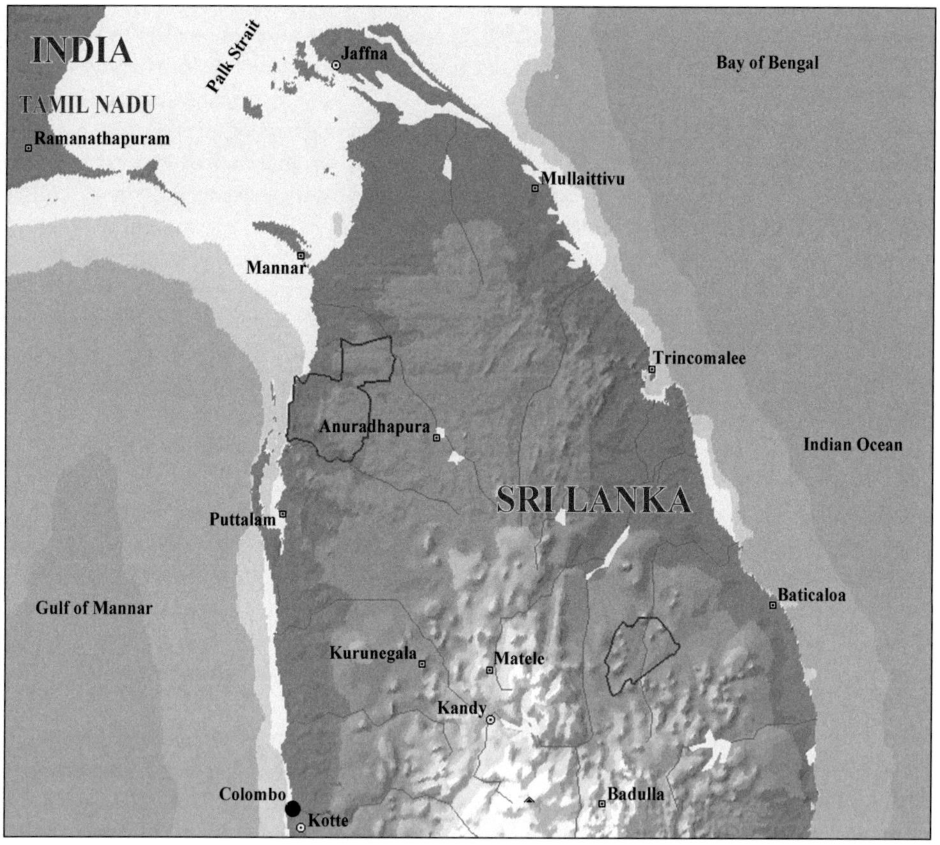

Map showing northern and eastern Sri Lanka – the parts of the country most impacted by the series of insurgencies, and then a civil war, that were to rage almost without interruption from 1971 until 2008. (Map by Tom Cooper)

Rohana Wijeweera, leader of the JVP. (Adrien Fontanellaz Collection)

and a 12-member politburo at the top. These controlled 19 district committees, each of which was lead by a district secretary. Militant cells were between 15 and 24 members strong, and attached to local and regional committees, which in turn were responsible to the district committees. Furthermore, the politburo controlled various commissions and sections, including one responsible for arms procurement and military training. However, this tightly structured organisation masked several crucial weaknesses. Foremost between these were deep rivalries between leaders of the party, and divisions within its membership. Geographic distances also proved detrimental to its cohesiveness. Finally, the significant growth the JVP experienced during the 1960s was foremost a result of a highly favourable social and economic contrast – rather than a well-thought-out and organised political strategy. The rural population was strained by unfavourable economic conditions and a 2.3% annual demographic growth, which generated high unemployment among the rural youth, despite its improved education. In a situation where Ceylonese society remained un-egalitarian by its nature, and where the elites inherited most of the economic and political positions from the British, youngsters struggled to find job opportunities and improve their status. Left without a choice, many turned to arms. Preparations for an armed struggle began in 1969, when the party's activists began collecting firearms, launched production of home-made bombs, and constructed several training camps. Outside the country, JVP's activists sought to establish contact with such communist countries as North Korea – though without success. Coupled with the lack of firearms and ammunition, this resulted in most of the training being rather theoretic by nature.[24]

Crack-Down on the JVP

Generally, the JVP's ideology was Maoist by nature, and its goal was to topple the government by force, and then form a radically new, equalitarian society. Its emphasis was on generating a support base in the countryside, but also in the cities, where it began conducting sustained political work. Although attempting to attract followers in the Tamil community – noticeably through promoting Tholilali Seydi (Workers News; a dedicated publication in the Tamil language) – the JVP always remained a Sinhalese movement. The point at which the JVP's leadership differed drastically from Maoist patterns was that it didn't expect a protracted armed struggle. On the contrary: emboldened by successful recruiting, the leaders of the party had arrived at the conclusion that a large-scale, but short insurrection would be perfectly enough to topple the government and seize power. Correspondingly, the JVP planned a nation-wide operation, including simultaneous attacks on police stations around the country, and an assault on the capital. The later part was a complex affair combining the assassination or capture of the Prime Minister, investments of the residences of key officials (like the Commander of Armed Forces or the Inspector General of the Police), Katunayake AB and the (Army's) Camp Panagoda, and the take-over of Radio Ceylon. These actions were to be combined with the seizure of the Kolonnawa Power Station, intended to cut off energy supply for Colombo and generate a blackout.

Related preparations did not go unnoticed. Already in 1969, the Police Special Branch Criminal Investigations Department had reported that the party was conducting secret meetings. Such reports were followed by hints of military preparations. Staffed by older officers, close to retirement and an end of their careers, the Police District Intelligence Bureau lacked the capacity to pursue more closely. Furthermore, there was latent distrust between different actors in the state apparatus, and this prevented the circulation of various reports about the JVP. Nevertheless, the police gradually began scrutinising JVP militants and arrested 104 of them in August 1970. Finally, the Ministry of Defence (MOD) had collected related intelligence: in 1967, and in 1969 again, one of its security advisors tasked with monitoring the JPV, collected different reports and correctly assessed the party's strategy and goals. Overall, as a whole, the state intelligence apparatus was foremost directed to monitor the traditional political parties, and only a few resources were allocated to monitoring the emerging threat of a communist insurgency.

Meanwhile, the political climate continued to deteriorate. On 27 February, the JVP launched several large rallies in Colombo, which culminated in a massive demonstration. On 6 March 1971, JVP militants and sympathisers staged a demonstration in front of the US Embassy, burned several cars, threw Molotov Cocktails in the direction of the embassy, and stabbed to death a police inspector. The police reacted by searching a house in Colombo where the Politburo was meeting, but most of its members made good their escape.

Four days later, four militants were killed while trying to assemble a bomb in Neludeniy. A similar incident occurred few days later again, this time at the Peradeniya University. Alerted by such incidents, the police launched a raid in the campus and found a large stock of bombs and associated materials – including more than 1,000 detonators. This prompted the government to order a general crack-down on the JVP. During dozens of raids run through the second half of March 1971, hundreds of militants were arrested, including Rohana Wijeweera, caught while touring district leaders of the movement. He was jailed at the local prison in Jaffna.

Activists that managed to escape were quick to re-organise. On 2 April 1971, nine leaders of the JVP met and decided to launch a general insurrection during the evening of 5 April. The already existing plan for the country-wide offensive was expanded through addition of a plan for attack on Jaffna prison, to free Wijeweera. All the local leaders were informed via coded telegram reading:

> 'JVP Appuhamy Expired. Funeral 5th'[25]

The Insurrection Week

Unsurprisingly, much of JVP's plan went awry almost immediately. It began with the local leader in Wellawaya misunderstanding his instructions and launching an isolated attack on the police station during the night from 4 to 5 April 1971 – fully 24 hours ahead of schedule. This set alarm bells ringing through headquarters of all of the security forces: military and the police were put on alert and prepared for action, while the government announced the proscription of the JVP, a nation-wide curfew, and then closed all schools and universities. The insurgents thus lost the crucial element of surprise.

Nevertheless, the JPV pushed on and launched its nation-wide operation during the evening of 5 April, as planned. It's most crucial efforts collapsed on their own, in a matter of a few minutes. Whether per chance or design, the police pre-empted the attack on Prime Minister Bandaranaike by raiding the house in which the involved militants were hiding. The other groups failed to appear, and thus all other attacks around Colombo failed to materialise. The two groups that assaulted the jail in Jaffna were quickly repulsed, while a 30-man strong group that attacked the nearby Jaffna police station failed to overrun it and lost several militants taken captive by the 10 police officers that defended the station.

Overall, between 5 and 9 April 1971, 93 out of 266 police stations around the country were attacked by groups from 25 to 30 militants, and thus it was the police that bore the brunt of the JVP's 'onslaught'. Eight of the stations were captured, together with minor quantities of firearms. For example, in the police station of Warakapola, attacked on 8 April, the communists captured two sub-machine guns and five rifles.

While run by highly motivated, but ill-trained and organised insurgents, and thus resulting in a mass of failures, these first actions sparked a larger upheaval among the rural youth, much of which ran alongside, instead in hand with actions of the communist militants. Some of these established groups of up to several hundreds of militants and launched their own attacks. At 0100 hrs of 7 April 1971, a large group of youngsters attacked the Polonnaruwa police station, defended by a few local police officers and a small detachment of the army. When the final assault was beaten back and the smoke cleared, around 0600 hrs, the defenders counted the bodies of 39 militants, and found six shotguns and around 500 makeshift bombs.

While most of the defenders were successful, the sheer pressure from such attacks forced the police to evacuate 43 stations and concentrate its forces at crucial locations. The JVP – and various groups that actually acted independently from it – were thus free to secure control of large areas, and even a few small towns. The insurgents immediately launched the work to establish their own para-state, noticeably by opening justice courts. Furthermore, they added to the chaos by felling trees to block roads, sabotaging the railway lines, and destroying telephone connections, thus isolating areas under their control from the external word.[26]

Turning the tide

Because of numerous interruptions of land connections, the MOD ordered the air force into action. Correspondingly, Doves and Herons of No. 2 Squadron, but also airliners of Air Ceylon, were mobilised to transport troops and supplies from Colombo to Trincomalee, Anuradhapura, Vavuniya, Ampara, Batticaloa and Jaffna. The three Jet Rangers and six pilots of No. 4 Helicopter Flight flew resupply missions, delivering ammunition and food to beleaguered police stations, while evacuating casualties on return flights. Jet Rangers also flew the first 'combat sorties' of the air force ever, when their crews – armed with Bren light machine guns and hand-grenades – attacked several of insurgent positions. Overall, in three days of action, the six pilots flew 122 hours in 73 sorties, delivering 16.5 tonnes of supplies. Realising that spares would not last long at this tempo of operations, Colombo issued an urgent request for help from the USA. Washington responded promptly, and a Lockheed C-141 StarLifter delivered the requested equipment to Katunayake AB on 12 April 1971.

Saladin armoured car of the 1st Reconnaissance Regiment SLA which were delivered after the 1971 insurgency. (Albert Grandolini Collection)

This Bell 206 was photographed while supporting construction work before the emergency of 1971 – but in a situation often experienced by Jet Ranger-crews in 1971, when they flew supplies for dozens of isolated police stations and military garrisons. (SLAF)

Even this was not enough. Indeed, although flying a staggering 12 hours a day, the three Jet Rangers were hopelessly insufficient for the task. Therefore, Colombo requested support from India and Pakistan, too. Despite raising tensions between the two, both countries reacted by deploying their detachments. Two Aerospatiale SE.316B Alouette III helicopters, and associated personnel, of the Pakistani Army arrived during the evening of 12 April. A 150 strong company of Ghurkhas arrived from India to bolster defences of Katunayake AB, the same evening, while a team of advisors led by Brigadier-General Ken Joshua followed the next day, together with six Alouettes of the Indian Air Force (IAF). Finally, the government of the USA donated six Bell 47G light helicopters to the RCyAF. After a five-day, crash conversion course, their pilots began to deploy them for CAS, armed with 7.62mm machine guns. Meanwhile, Jet Provosts mothballed at China Bay AB, were hastily put back into service, and flew their first air strikes against JVP-controlled buildings using 7.62mm Browning machine guns, and British-made, 60lb unguided rockets.[27]

By 13 April 1971, the security forces had reorganised themselves. Their operations were meanwhile coordinated by a single body, commanded by Major-General Attygalle. At this moment in time the JVP lost the initiative because, after the failure of its all-out attempt against the government, its leadership lacked any 'Plan B'. Unsurprisingly, the security forces began advancing and reasserting control over the lost areas. Progressively, they retook most of the towns – like Anuradhapura, on 18 April; Kagalle and Eliptiya on 21 April, and Deniyawa, on 24 April. Furthermore, the RCA made good use of its COIN training to conduct aggressive patrols and set up ambushes on locations where insurgent activity was reported. Foremost, the police paid attention to organise civilian vigilance committees in specific areas, to bolster the work of security services through provision of timely intelligence. JPV insurgents not only proved unable to face regular army troops in combat, but tended to panic when on receiving end of mortar fire, especially at night.

Although its conduct of operations was generally effective, repression by government forces against the local population was fierce. Thousands were arrested and several hundreds summarily executed. By the end of April 1971, the die-hard militants were thus forced to withdraw to remote areas, where only a few scattered groups managed to remain active until the end of the year. When the government offered a general amnesty, this was widely accepted. The last few JVP insurgents surrendered after more than 500,000 leaflets were dropped by RCyAF aircraft, between 29 April and 3 May 1971.

Altogether, by the end of June 1971, the security services had killed, captured or accepted the surrender of 16,000 JVP insurgents. In turn, they suffered 376 casualties, including 53 servicemen killed in action (KIA). The police alone had suffered 37 KIA and 193 wounded in action (WIA). Exactly how many were killed in total remains unknown: the exact number of civilians killed by both sides remains unavailable, while published accounts range from 1,200 to as many as 50,000.[28]

During the following years, the government reacted by significantly expanding the police: from 10,605 in 1971, to nearly 20,000 by 1979. However, it failed to draw several crucial lessons, foremost of which was that it took no actions to improve the performance of various intelligence services. This was to have disastrous repercussions during the following decade, when the security forces were to fail in their attempts to eliminate the first Tamil insurgent groups while these were still in their infancy and hence, highly vulnerable.[29]

The Boys

The first cases of violence perpetrated by the Tamils occurred during the riots of 1956 and 1958. These were low-scale, spontaneous affairs. For example, in 1956, eleven Tamils armed with rifles fired at Sinhalese civilians. In 1958, two police officers were killed in the Batticaloa area, and one group derailed a train. During the unrest of 1961, the army attacked a few armed groups of the Tamils at the Jaffna Peninsula, but neither side suffered casualties.

Later the same year, some 20 sympathisers of the Federal Party had created their own group, the Pulip Padai (Army of Tigers). Their activities remained limited to distributing pamphlets that advocated the creation of a Tamil Eelam as the sole solution for Tamil's plights. The Army of Tigers disappeared during the second half of the 1960s, though, and a new group – the Tamil Liberation Organisation (TLO) – came into being in Jaffna in 1969. Centred on a core of only 10 militants armed with revolvers, this group ventured into the dangerous trade of bomb-making – and promptly suffered several casualties.

Nadraraja Thangavelu (alias Thangadurai), co-founder of the TELO. (TELO, via wikicommons)

As an ever increasing number of students became politically active and joined such organisations as the Tamil Student League or the Tamil Youth League, the movement continued to grow. In 1977, the TLO re-named itself the Tamil Eelam Liberation Organisation (TELO) and created an 'official' armed wing: the Tamil Eelam Liberation Army (TELA). Encouraged by the early success of the JVP, and by the independence of Bangladesh, in 1971, the TELO and TELA opted for an armed struggle. Several other small armed groups appeared as well. Curiously, the appearance of the same was regarded with sympathy by several Tamil politicians, who considered their small-scale actions 'complementary' to their own activities, and rather benevolently called them, 'the Boys'. The Police took no chances: informed about the appearance of Tamil militants, it raided their homes in 1972 and 1973. While many activists were arrested, this only resulted in putting them all in touch with each other – in jail, where they received the opportunity to exchange ideas about the best way for achieving an independent Tamil Eelam.

The most active of 'the Boys' was the group led by Ponnudarai Sivakumaran, and thus known as the 'Sivakumaran Group'. Between 1970 and 1971, this launched several assassination attempts, notably against Alfred Durippah, the mayor of Jaffna, who was a Tamil but considered a 'traitor' because of his SFLP-membership. While escaping death or detention on several occasions, Sivakumaran's luck run out on 5 June 1974, when an attempted bank robbery resulted in him finding himself surrounded by the police. Still only 17, he was determined not to be captured alive and committed suicide by swallowing a cyanide pill he carried with him for precisely such an eventuality. As a result, Sivakumaran became widely revered as the first major martyr of the Tamil struggle for independence: his 'no surrender' became a model for countless other Tamil militants.[30]

The Tiger of Velvittiturai

In January 1975, a group of young Tamil expatriates created the Eelam Revolutionary Organisation (EROS) in London, in Great Britain. They quickly established connections to several similar organisations in Europe – including the Irish Republican Army (IRA). Correspondingly, EROS militants underwent bomb-making training in Sweden, run by operatives of the IRA, while three of their members travelled to Beirut, in Lebanon, where they underwent a six-month training course by the Palestinian Liberation Organisation (PLO).

Meanwhile, another nascent armed group appeared, which was to have a decisive influence during the subsequent decades: the Tamil New Tigers (TNT) was established in 1972, by a small group of militants centred on Velupillai Pirabhakaran. On 27 July of the same year, accompanied by three other militants, Pirabhakaran assassinated Alfred Durippah in a temple, and fled with his victim's car. This action made the TNT famous in all of Jaffna. On 5 March 1976, his group attacked the People's Bank of Puttur, and escaped with a haul worth 700,000 Sri Lankan Rupees (LKR), including about 500,000 in cash. Finally, on 5 May 1976, the group renamed itself the Liberation Tigers of Tamil Eelam (LTTE), and adopted an emblem drawn by the leader himself: a Tiger head – a symbol often used by Tamil warrior kings in the past – surrounded by 33 cartridges.[31]

Born in November 1954 to a prominent, middle-class family in Velvittiturai, a quiet town on the Jaffna Peninsula well known for smuggling activities, Pirabhakaran developed a strong passion for reading in his childhood. He became a keen reader of comics, the Mahabharata Hindu epic, Tamil historical novels, and books about the

A very rare photo of a young Velupillai Pirabhakaran. (LTTE via Adrien Fontanellaz)

life of such as Subhas Chandra Bose and Napoleon Bonaparte.[32] In the meantime, he started training himself, honing his marksmanship by hunting with airguns, and developing physical stamina. Losing interest in further education, Pirabhakaran became ever deeper involved in militancy, and attracted the attention of the police for the first time in 1972. Still only 18 years old, he was already well-trained for what was to follow, and thus quickly disappeared into a clandestine existance after having burned all existing photographs to make himself harder to recognize. He changed his hideouts very often, and never spoke about his plans with anyone. Foremost, he proved meticulous and patient, and capable of cautiously planning for weeks, even months in advance, whenever necessary.

Later on, Pirabhakaran had a book about Che Guevara translated by his militants into the Tamil language (he never spoke any other language but Tamil). However, he never developed much interest in such leftist theoreticians as Marx, Lenin or Mao: instead, Pirabhakaran always emphasised armed action over political works. Correspondingly, and contrary to the usual practice for 'classic', Marxist-Leninist movements, the organisation he gradually developed eventually became a military with a political wing. When an intellectual tried to argue with him about priorities of political work, Pirabhakaran offered a very clear answer:

> We have to act first, people will follow us then [...] You intellectuals are afraid of blood. No struggle will take place without killing. What do you want me to do? You people live in comfort and try to prove me wrong. So what should I do? Take cyanide and die?

Rise of the LTTE

The most active Tamil insurgent group in the period between the mid-1970s and late 1983 were the TELO, the PLOTE and the LTTE. They had only a few dozens of militants each, lacked arms and equipment, and were supported by a diminutive part of the Tamil population. In particular, the nascent LTTE remained a close-knit group of youngsters from Velvittiturai and Point Pedro, hand-picked by Pirabhakaran after careful checks of their backgrounds. Once accepted, most of newcomers had to adopt an alias to hide their backgrounds.[33] Between 1976 and 1980, Anton Balasingham, Sathasivan Krishnakumar (alias Kittu), Kadirgamapillai Nallainathan (alias Uma Maheshwaran), Gopalasamy Mahendrarajah (alias Mahattaya), Charles Lucas

Pirabhakaran with a sub-machine gun, in 1984. (Rohan Gunaratna)

Anthony (alias Seelan), Sathasivam Sivashanmugamoorthy (alias Sundaram), and Kambarmalai Sattiyanathan (alias Shankar) joined the LTTE. Seelan, a young man from Trincomalee, became the virtual deputy of Pirabhakaran, whenever the latter was absent from Jaffna. Balasingham – a Marxist intellectual married to Adele, an Australian nurse – became the movement's primary political theoretician and chief negotiator. Each of them had to swear an oath of allegiance and was submitted to a drastic code that forbade – among others – any sexual intercourse outside marriage. Furthermore, the group was instructed to strictly avoid making use of civilian property owned by the Tamil, without providing at least some compensation.[34]

For most of 1976 and 1977, the LTTE was busy with organising a network of safe houses and thus kept a low profile. A training camp was set up in a small and isolated farm, a few kilometres outside Vavuniya, and a few other, minor training facilities elsewhere in northern Sri Lanka. Thanks to connections established via the EROS, two of LTTE's militants were sent for three months of training with the PLO in Lebanon, but this experience proved a disappointment, foremost because it did not open a source of military-grade firearms – as expected. Meanwhile, insurgent actions resembled those of banditry: attacks on banks, targeted assassinations, or small-scale ambushes against local police officers, informants, or Tamil politicians considered 'traitors'. However, even these small groups always maintained one small, but critical, advantage that proved decisive for their survival: the ability to cross the Palk Strait aboard small boats operated by smugglers, whenever in need of refuge. In other cases,

Charles Lucas Anthony, alias Seelan. (LTTE via wikicommons)

Uma Maheshwaran, leader of the PLOTE. (Adrien Fontanellaz Collection)

they would flee to the nearby Indian state of Tamil Nadu, where the local police ignored them on condition they did not create trouble. Thus, and despite several important setbacks, all the groups grew ever more audacious. Over time, they began attacking even isolated outposts of the Sri Lankan armed forces and police stations. This was especially the case with the LTTE that, despite its tiny size, even began interfering local elections in 1983.[35]

In 1979, the LTTE went through a crisis caused by a confrontation between Pirabhakaran and Uma Maheshwaran – triggered by a love affair between the latter and a female militant. Fiercely insisting on a strict application of the group's code of conduct – and also keen to sack the political leader – Pirabhakaran finally got what he wanted:

Official crest of the PLOTE. (Adrien Fontanellaz Collection)

Uma Maheshwaran was expelled. However, this affair diminished his own authority, too. Disgusted, Pirabhakaran left the LTTE and joined the TELO, where he served as instructor in a training camp in Tamil Nadu for nearly a year – before returning to Sri Lanka to resume his position as, this time uncontested, leader of the LTTE.

Uma Maheshwaran did not stay idle: along with several ex-Tigers who had followed him after his expulsion, he created his own group, the People's Liberation Organization of Tamil Eelam (PLOTE) in 1980, based in the Killinochchi area. Soon, the LTTE and the PLOTE became fierce opponents and on 2 January 1982, Seelan killed Sundaram – the latter group's highly efficient military leader – in a shoot-out in Jaffna. Determined to extract revenge, Uma Maheshwaran travelled to Madras with two other militants, searching for an opportunity to kill his LTTE counterpart. On 19 May 1982, the two leaders, escorted by bodyguards, ran into each other at the Pondy Bazaar, and immediately opened fire with revolvers. Both were arrested by the local police and jailed. Fortunately for them, the authorities of Tamil Nadu proved rather lenient – if not outright supportive – and placed them in a house arrest in different places, instead of sending them back to Sri Lanka, as requested by Colombo. Their mutual feud went on, of course.

Starting in the early 1980s, dozens of additional Tamil insurgent groups began to appear – to a degree where there was certainly an inflation of such groups.[36] Most of them were hopelessly ineffective. Sole exception to this was the Eelam People's Revolutionary Liberation Front (EPRLF). Established in 1981, and organised along classic Leninist patterns, this included several front organisations preoccupied with gaining popular support. The EPRLF also established a dedicated armed wing – the People's Liberation Army (PLA) – which became active in April 1983. Overall, the EPRLF, TELO, EROS, LTTE, and PLOTE thus became what was commonly known as 'the big five' – most important players on the Tamil insurgent scene.

Table 5: The Big Five and Other Tamil Insurgent Groups, 1960s-1980s[37]

Designation	Notes
TELO, Tamil Eelam Liberation Organisation	Est. 1969, named TLO until 1977
LTTE, Liberation Tigers of Tamil Eelam	Est. 1972 as TNT, re-named LTTE in 1976
EROS, Eelam Revolutionary Organisation	Est. 1975
PLOTE, People's Liberation Organisation of Tamil Eelam	Est. 1980
EPRLF, Eelam People's Revolutionary Liberation Front	Est. 1981
TEA, Tamil Eelam Army	
TELE, Tamil Eelam Liberation Extremists	
TERO, Tamil Eelam Revolutionary Organisation	
TERPLA, Tamil Eelam Revolutionary People's Liberation Army	
RFTE, Red Front of Tamil Eelamists	
TELG, Tamil Eelam Liberation Guerrillas	
NLFTE, National Liberation Front of Tamil Eelam	
IFTA, I Lanka Freedom Tamil Army	
TEDF, Tamil Eelam Defence Front	
TENA, Tamil Eelam National Army	
TPSO, Tamil People's Security Organisation	
TPSF, Tamil People's Security Front	
TEC, Tamil Eelam Commando	
TELF, Tamil Eelam Liberation Front	
TEEF, Tamil Eelam Eagles Front	
GATE, Guerrilla Army of Tamil Eelam	
RCG, Red Crescent Guerillas	
EM, Eagle Movement	
SRSL, Socialist Revolutionary Social Liberation	
TEBM, Tamil Eelam Blood Movement	
TPCU, Tamil People's Command Unit	
ELT, Eelam Liberation Tigers	
TLDF, Tamil Liberation Defence Front	
RELO, Revolutionary Eelam Liberation Organisation	
TESS, Tamil Eelam Security Service	
PLP, People's Liberation Army	
TPDF, Tamil People's Democratic Front	
TELC, Tamil Eelam Liberation Cobras	
TS, Three Stars	

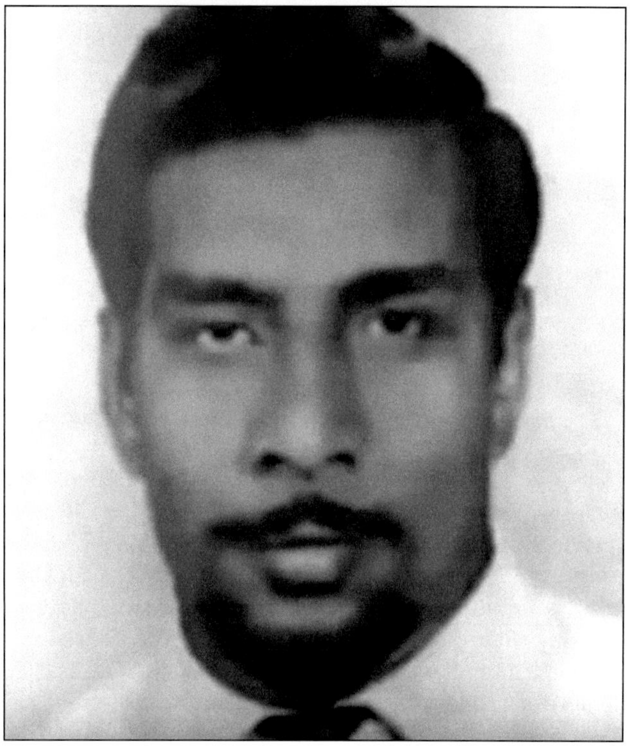

Anton Balasingham joined the LTTE in the second half of the 1970s. (Adrien Fontanellaz)

Hunt for Police Officers

The LTTE and TELO initially concentrated their actions against the local police forces and their informants, in a deliberate effort to break the government forces' ability to gather intelligence about them. In the meantime, both groups conducted several bank attacks to get the necessary funds. On 15 August 1977, LTTE gunmen shot dead at least three policemen and injured a fourth during separate incidents, but this was only the beginning: 1978 was to prove even more deadly for the police forces. On 7 April 1978, the CID's Inspector Bastiampillai travelled to an isolated location in the Mannar district with two other policemen and a driver. A Tamil himself, the Inspector was widely considered as ruthless, but also renowned for his knowledge about the militant groups, and had correspondingly being informed of the possible presence of an insurgent training camp in the Murunkan area. The three agents soon met with a small group of young men near a well, who turned out to be members of the LTTE. Successfully pretending to be local farmers, the Tigers waited for opportune moment, and then one of them seized the inspector's sub-machine gun and opened fire. In ensuing fire-fight, the three police officers and their driver were killed and their bodies dumped in the countryside. To add insult to injury, on 6 May, a small group of TELO hitmen assaulted the house of Inspector Pathmanathan, another authority about militant groups, and killed him.

In June 1978, Inspector Kumaru was assassinated in Jaffna, while on the morning of 5 December, six LTTE militants attacked the People's Bank in Thinnelveli and killed two police officers and wounded a third, before escaping with bags filled with LKR 1.18 million.

The attacks continued in 1979, and by mid-July 1979, the government acknowledged that 14 policemen had been killed by the militants. Significantly, the LTTE became renowned for attacks launched by militants riding bicycles, while the 'signature' of the TELO hitmen were head-shots from a very close range.

The insurgents also continued to target Tamil politicians considered as traitors. On 25 January 1978, Pirabhakaran and Uma Maheshwaran attempted to kill a Tamil MP in Colombo, because he rallied for the UNP. On 7 September 1978, two militants boarded the

Wreckage of the Avro 748 destroyed by a time-bomb planted by two LTTE insurgents, on 7 September 1978. (Albert Grandolini Collection)

Air Ceylon's Avro 748 registered as 4R-ACJ, for a flight from Palali to Ratmalana. On arrival, they exited the aircraft with other passengers, but left behind a time-bomb set to detonate once the aircraft would be airborne. Fortunately for the crew and passengers, the bomb went off prematurely, while the Avro was still on the ground. However, the destruction of the valuable aircraft broke the back of Air Ceylon, which was already suffering severe financial problems: the company closed less than one year later.[38]

Although limited in numbers, the assassinations of police officers and informants gradually achieved their aim. The Inspector General of Police Stanley Senayake, explained that his service became,

> ... unable to make any headway in investigations. The local population is too terrorised to give any information!

A major problem was that the authorities underestimated the challenge presented by the militants, and considered these as 'acts of civil disorder'. An infantry battalion was deployed on the Jaffna Peninsula for a few weeks in August 1977, to back-up the police. However, no significant action was taken before the Parliament adopted the Prevention of Terrorist Act (PTA), on 19 July 1979, and expanded the prerogatives of the security forces, allowing them – amongst others – to detain suspects for up to 18 months without a trial. Furthermore, the entire 1st RR was deployed in the north, with one of its squadrons in Vavuniya, Anuradhapura, Mankulam, and Jaffna each, while Brigadier-General Tissa Indraka Weeratunga – also known as 'Bull Weeratunga' – was appointed the Commander of Security Forces in the North. The order he received from the President was crystal clear:

> It will be your duty to eliminate, in accordance with the laws of this land, the menace of terrorism in all its form... The Task has to be performed by you and completed before 31 December 1979.

Bull Weeratunga ordered the army and the police into action immediately: in a general and massive crack-down, hundreds of youngster Tamils were arrested, torture applied on a large scale, while – often mutilated – bodies of the 'disappeared' were dumped around the countryside. While this ruthless action proved effective in the short term, it was to prove disastrous in the long term. Most of insurgent leaders were forced to flee to Tamil Nadu and the ability of even such groups as the TELO and the LTTE to conduct attacks on Sri Lanka were drastically reduced. However, the brutalities by the security forces not only served the militant propaganda, but also bolstered their ranks with hundreds of refugees. Furthermore, in accordance with his order, Bull Weeratunga ended his operation on 31 December 1979, and the SLA's presence was subsequently reduced to the earlier level of one battalion.[39]

Escalation

The TELO, the LTTE and the PLOTE were all back to northern Sri Lanka by early 1981. Indeed, the combined number of attacks by these three groups alone superseded the total number of all attacks from 1978 and 1979. The intensity of their operations then continued to rise, as – except for police officers – they began to attack members of the military, too. The most daring operation by the TELO was undertaken on 25 March 1981, when its militants ambushed a vehicle carrying LKR7.8 million about 20 kilometres outside Point Pedro, and killed two police officers before disappearing with all the money. That group's luck run out on 5 April of the same year, when it's two leaders – Nadraraja Thangavelu (alias Thangadurai), and Selvaraja Yogachandran (alias Kuttimani) were arrested while attempting to take a boat for a trip to Tamil Nadu. Their arrest triggered the capture of 24 other militants, which resulted in a de-facto destruction of this group.

The PLOTE was meanwhile assassinating police officers and Tamil MPs in the Killinochchi area. On 31 July 1981, one of its groups overran the Annakottai police station, where it killed two police officers and seized 23 firearms and 1,500 rounds of ammunition. On 29 October, the PLOTE robbed cash and jewellery worth LKR40 million from the People's Bank in Killinochchi, and killed a corporal from the 2nd (V) GW.

However, meanwhile the SLA had activated a small intelligence cell with Tamil speaking officers. Despite the lack of support of the army hierarchy – which even refused to allocate funds (and thus forced the involved officers to use their personal funds to cover part of their related expenses) – the intelligence team proved highly efficient. As a result, the SLA launched "Operation Round Up" and arrested nearly 30 insurgents, including 12 hardcore militants in November 1981. In February 1982, the army captured Anton Ampalagam, one of PLOTE's leaders, the interrogation of whom resulted in the arrest of multiple additional militants. Nevertheless, the group continued launching attacks on military officers and other ranks well into the Year 1983.[40]

However, the largest number of attacks during this period was launched by the LTTE, who meanwhile considered the destruction of the law enforcement system as its absolute priority. On 15 October 1981, a LTTE outfit led by Seelan attacked the SLA for the first time, and ambushed a jeep of the Sri Lanka Army Works Services on the Stanley road in Jaffna. Corporals Hewawasam and Tissera, the two servicemen killed during the attack were the first SLA casualties of the war.

On 2 July 1982, a group led by Shankar set up another road ambush, this time against a police vehicle, and killed four, while wounding three. On 27 October of the same year, Seelan led a well-organised attack against the Chavakachcheri police station. While a first cover group blocked the A9 road to delay eventual reinforcements, an assault group invested the station and swiftly seized it, killing three agents in the process. Three militants – including Seelan – were wounded during this action, but the LTTE thus captured 33 rifles and two sub-machine guns. This operation gave even more handsome dividends when the Police decided to close more than half of its stations in the Jaffna Peninsula, thus weakening further its already shrinking control over the area. Left untouched by the waves of arrests which had touched TELO and PLOTE during the two previous years, the LTTE was the only insurgent group which remained active by the end of 1982, although it had suffered is first casualty on 27 November 1982 when Shankar died in an hospital in Tamil Nadu from a wound suffered during a gunfight with Sri Lanka security forces a few days earlier. In revenge, the LTTE gunmen killed Inspector Wijawardene and his driver in an ambush at Point Pedro, on 18 April 1983, while a

Ruins of the Jaffna Library, torched by the Sri Lankan police on 16 August 1981. (Adrien Fontanellaz Collection)

group of Tigers ambushed a SLA convoy in the vicinity of Paranthan, on 4 March, and claimed to have damaged two armoured cars and wounded five soldiers. Eventually, the situation reached a point where the army was forced to deploy additional infantry forces in a series of small bases near Palali, Guruagar, Thondamannaru, Velvittiturai, Madagal, Point Pedro, Pooneryn, and Elephant Pass, in 1983.[41]

Despite the increasing audacity and sophistication of their actions, the insurgents remained very few in numbers. As of mid-1983, their totals had been assessed at between 200 and 300 – for all movements – of which a core of about 30 were involved in most of actions. It cannot be sufficiently emphasised that the majority of their victims were Tamils. However, and for reasons that played straight into their hands, their actions – and consequences of the same – were far out of proportion.

The legal Tamil opposition, foremost the TULF, failed to make any significant advance, and thus lost its credibility within the Tamil population. Indeed, the LTTE meanwhile felt strong enough to assassinate a TULF member of parliament that criticised them, on 22 February 1983, while – capitalising on the general disillusion – the group then enforced a boycott of local elections in May of the same year. When the TULF attempted to stage a political meeting, this was dispersed by several Tigers that fired into the air. During the elections, on 18 May, the group led by Seelan also attacked a polling station in Jaffna, killing on soldier of the Army. The result was that only about 10% of the population of the Northern Province managed to vote.

Furthermore, attacks by the Tamil militants triggered waves of anti-Tamil violence. Many of these were initiated by undisciplined police officers and members of the military, but each of them further widened the gap between the Sinhalese and the Tamils, further diminished the TULF authority, and increased the stance of the militants. One of most severe of such incidents occurred on 16 August 1981, when the PLOTE's assassination of two police officers triggered a fierce retaliation by the police in Jaffna: this not only destroyed the TULF's main office, the headquarters of a major Tamil newspaper, and several shops, but also burned the Jaffna Public Library, where over 90,000 ancient manuscripts were lost. Two months later, the burial of two police officers triggered another wave of anti-Tamil riots in the Western and Eastern provinces. By this time, the discipline of the Sri Lankan police officers in Jaffna experienced a complete break-down: many of them had actually been re-deployed away from their usual areas of operations and thus not only lacked training but were also unaccustomed to the conditions prevailing in Jaffna.[42]

The military was not immune to similar unravelling of the discipline. On the contrary, random reprisals followed every militant attack, and peaked in the rampage of the soldiers of the 1st Rajarata Rifles in Jaffna, on 18 May 1983: in the course of that action, several of troops opened fire even on a truck carrying officers dispatched to attempt to reassert discipline – although without causing further casualties. The subsequent court of inquiry sacked a sergeant and three corporals, responsible for the break-down of the discipline. More than 90 troops deserted in protests, in turn incensing the Army's hierarchy that then sacked all the officers present at their base in Anuradhapura on the day the troops deserted. Eventually, the Rajarata Rifles Regiment was disbanded on 14 October 1983, and its remaining troops amalgamated with the Vijayabahu Infantry Regiment. In turn, officers and other ranks from these two units were drawn to form the Gajaba Infantry Regiment, a few months later.[43]

CHAPTER 4
BLACK JULY

A chain of events that was to completely change the character of the Sri Lankan conflict began on 15 July 1983. On that day, an army detachment was ordered into a village outside Jaffna, on the basis of intelligence that Seelan would be around. Indeed, the notorious LTTE's hitman and two other militants were there – and taken by surprise by the appearance of well-armed troops. They attempted to flee across rice fields, with soldiers in hot pursuit. Still working on an injury suffered during an earlier clash, Seelan was slow: determined not to be captured alive, he ordered one of the other two militants to shoot him in the head.

Black July

Seething with rage, Pirabhakaran mobilised the core of the LTTE, and prepared them for an ambush of the Army. Thanks to his expanded network of informants, he identified a perfect site near the Jaffna University: this provided a good killing ground and was known to be crossed by an army patrol of two vehicles from the nearby Camp Gurunagar, every day between 2300 and 2400 hrs local time. The leader of the LTTE and ten of his Tigers, all armed with G-3 and AKM assault rifles, laid their ambush on the evening of 23 July: a massive, remotely-controlled mine was planed next to the road, and the killing ground covered from four firing positions.

On the same day, a rotation had taken place in the Camp Gurunagar; soldiers of the 1st SLLI relieved their counterparts from the 1st Sinha Battalion. A 15-man strong patrol of the 1st SLLI – codenamed Four Four Bravo, and commanded by 2nd Lieutenant de Vas Gunawardena – moved out for its usual round along a well-established pattern: a jeep followed by a truck. Things did not go exactly along the LTTE's plan: the remote detonator was activated too early, and the mine went off under the jeep – instead under the truck. The bulk of the troops was thus shaken and shocked, but still found the time to open fire and lob grenades at the insurgents firing at them. The situation thus degenerated into a fierce fire-fight, in which one insurgent was killed. However, surrounded and exposed in the killing zone, the troops fell one after the other. Eventually, only two survived, and one of them subsequently died of his wounds. The LTTE thus captured 12 assault rifles, two machine guns, and a shotgun.[44]

A SLAF transport brought the bodies of the killed troops to Colombo for a collective burial, on 24 July. The related ceremony provided the spark for massive anti-Tamil riots that raged through the city for the rest of the night – even more so because the police remained inactive and sometimes even took part in the exactions. In the course of those frenzied hours, hundreds of shops and houses owned by the Tamils were set on fire, and dozens were killed. Ethnic violence surpassed anything that had happened before, and turned into an outright pogrom: 20 Tamils were burned alive in a mini-bus and 52 Tamil detainees of the Colombo's Wellikade Prison (including two TELO leaders) were killed by Sinhalese prisoners, before the violence spread into virtually the entire Central and Southern Provinces. The SLN managed to restore order in Trincomalee, but

Typical SLA patrol of the early 1980s consisted of a general-purpose vehicle ('jeep') and a truck carrying a platoon of troops, exactly as in this photograph. (Albert Grandolini Collection)

The 'Black July' riots of 24 July 1983, saw massive anti-Tamil riots by an enraged mob that torched entire streets of Colombo, murdering almost everybody in its way. (Albert Grandolini Collection)

Wreckage of a minibus in the aftermath of rioting in Columbo on the evening of 24 July 1983. (Albert Grandolini Collection)

Another sad scene of anti-Tamil riots and pogrom from Black July 1983. (Albert Grandolini Collection)

was forced to dishonourably discharge 81 sailors that took part in the pogroms. By the time the dust and smoke cleared, between 600 and 1,000 Tamils were murdered, 8,077 cases of arson and 3,835 cases of looting were recorded.

The first consequence of the Black July riots was to widen enormously the existing gap between the Sri Lankan Tamil and Sinhalese communities. The small Sinhalese community in the north, which had not been targeted by the militants so far, feared reprisals and began to resettle in the centre and the south of the island. Economic consequences were severe also because the number of tourists visiting the island was reduced to a trickle while several foreign corporations shelved important investments programs in the country. Furthermore, the volume of the foreign development aid dropped sharply in the following years. Indeed, while the previous riots had been largely unnoticed in the World, the Black July riots hit the headlines there.

In northern Sri Lanka, dozens of thousands of the Tamils fled to Tamil Nadu. Many fled all the way to the West, where significant Tamil communities had already settled during the previous decades. By the end of 1983, around 100,000 Tamils were registered as living in Australia, Great Britain, Canada, New Zealand, and the USA alone. After Black July, large numbers among these expatriates began to donate funds to the various militant movements at home. Furthermore, the refugees staying in camps in northern Sri Lanka or in Tamil Nadu proved a very fertile recruitment ground for the Insurgents.[45]

The Indian Factor

The Black July riots triggered a massive wave of protest in Tamil Nadu and this had nearly immediate repercussions on the Indian government – then led by Prime Minister Indira Gandhi. Indeed, Indira Gandhi's Congress Party was electorally weak in South-India and therefore relied on alliances with local political forces. In Tamil Nadu, these forces were the Dravida Munnetra Kashagam Party (DMK) and the All India-Ana Dravida Munnetra Kashagam (AI-ADMK), led by Muthuvelu Karunanidhi and Marudur Gopalan Ramachandran, respectively. Both parties were sympathetic to the Sri Lankan Tamil cause, thus reflecting the mood among the Indian Tamil populations. They were fiercely opposed to each other too and prone to accuse their rival of lack of support to the Sri Lanka Tamils. Hence, for internal political reasons, it was necessary for Indira Gandhi to do something about the Sri Lankan crisis.

There were several further factors enticing New Delhi into an intervention – aside from notorious personal antipathy between the Prime Ministers of India and Sri Lanka. Governments of Sri Lanka became a major source of concern for New Delhi in 1971, when they authorised the transport aircraft of the Pakistan Air Force to make refuelling stops during the Indo-Pakistani War. Things only worsened once J. R. Jayewardene rose to power in 1977: his UNP-dominated government turned drastically from the self-sufficient economic policy followed by the SFLP, to market-oriented reforms associated with a shift from a strictly neutralist stance toward a more pro-Western policy. Furthermore, the Sri Lankan government contracted a US-led consortium to refurbish Trincomalee Oil Tanks Farm and allowed the Voice of America radio to establish a station on the Island. The Indians immediately suspected that these could be the beginning of an American presence in the highly strategic Trincomalee harbour, and that the Voice of America station was a cover for an ELINT facility targeting India. Such a US presence in the 'strategic backyard' of the neutralist India's was anathema for New Delhi, where most of the politicians were still recalling the deployment of the US Navy's carrier battle group centred on nuclear-powered aircraft carrier USS *Enterprise* (CVN-65) in the Gulf of Bengal, and various threats expressed against India during the Indo-Pakistani War of 1971. Finally, at least from Indira Gandhi's perspective, the riots of 1983 were also a good opportunity to teach the politicians in Colombo a lesson.

Tamil militant Kuloppodi Kumar, seen in a photograph taken during his training by the Palestinians in the Beka'a Valley. (Rohan Gunaratna)

Although the option of an outright invasion might have been on the table at some point, re-enacting what India did in the former Eastern Pakistan – then Bangladesh – of 1971, through provision of support for Sri Lankan Tamil insurgents, was out of the question.[46] Indeed, such an adventure could easily backfire inside India, because of several secessionist movements were active in India. Therefore, the government in New Delhi opted for a two-sided strategy:

- 1.) Indian diplomacy was ordered to mediate between Colombo and the insurgents, with the aim of reaching a peace agreement that would stop the violence and thus satisfy the local Tamil population, though without granting them independence.
- 2.) Covert support was to be provided to Tamil insurgents, but in limited amounts only: just enough to enable the militants to continue harassing the armed forces of Sri Lanka, but not enough to defeat them. The resulting military pressure was to be used to force Colombo into concessions.

Over time, such Indian plots were to prove a reason for much frustration between insurgents, once they realised they were being played within the wider context of Indian strategic interests.[47]

Building-up the insurgency

The responsibility to train and arm the militants fell on the Research and Analysis Wing (RAW), the Indian external intelligence agency, which had been created in 1968, and already maintained contacts to several of the groups. Once this became known between the Tamil youngsters, many of these – already incensed by Black July – volunteered to rally to the different militant organisations. A cadre from the PLOTE commented later:

> Until then, I had found it difficult to bring people into the movement. From then on, there was such a rush for joining our struggle that I found it difficult to control the crowds.[48]

By the end of 1983, RAW had set a training camp in the vicinity of Dehradun and had recruited officers of the Indian Army to act as instructors. Militants were sent there to follow three to six-month long courses where they were trained in guerrilla warfare. Training included the use of small radio stations ('walkie-talkies') and of various firearms and land mines. Separate and more specialised courses were

Following Black July, the Indian intelligence service, RAW, began providing arms to different Tamil insurgency groups. Correspondingly, Sri Lankan security forces began finding ever larger arms caches during their raids in the north of the country. (Albert Grandolini Collection)

Pirabhakaran (right) with M. G. Ramachandran, Chief Minister of the Indian Federal State of Tamil Nadu, in 1984. (Adrien Fontanellaz)

also provided to small groups of carefully-selected militants about intelligence gathering and combat diving. A handful of militants were trained into the use of heavy machine guns (HMGs). The output of the Dehradun camp was rather limited as the total number of insurgents trained there between 1983 and 1987 is estimated to around 1,000, including approximately 200 from the LTTE and 200 from the EPRLF. Opting for a 'divide and rule' policy, and trying to balance its aid to prevent one of the groups becoming more prominent, the RAW took great care to deal with each Tamil group separately, and not to train militants from different organisations at the same time. Furthermore, Indian intelligence exploited this opportunity to infiltrate several of the groups and collect as much information about them as possible, while in turn preventing them from establishing links to other potential sources of support from abroad.

Unsurprisingly, the few Tamil militants which had previously been trained in Lebanon – by the PLO and by the Popular Front for the Liberation of Palestine (PFLP) – were critical of the quality of training provided by the Indians, noticeably because Palestinian instructors were experienced fighters and had even taken with them a few trainees in operation against the Israelis. Furthermore, most of the Tamil militants had ideologies more similar to those of the Palestinian militants than to any average Indian Army officer. A militant of the EROS commented:

> The Palestinians considered everyone as equals. The Indians were different. They were the we-know-all types.[49]

Another was even more direct in his commentary, relating,

> Two of us had been trained by the PLO. We knew that what the Indians were teaching us was useless stuff.[50]

Even so, the RAW-organised training was only the tip of the iceberg. Namely, the Indians left several of the Tamil militant groups to organise their own training camp in Tamil Nadu, and then with support of the local authorities. The instructors were either militants who had been trained in Dehradun, or retired Indian military officers and other ranks. By early 1986, according the Tamil Nadu Director General of Police, there were no fewer than 45 camps with various capacities, operated by 12 different Tamil insurgent groups. These were training a total of 3,363 militants at the same time, as detailed in Table 6. Significantly, the 'big five' alone controlled 38 out of these 45 camps, and were training 3,139 militants – or around 93% of the total number of Sri Lankan Tamils trainees present in Tamil Nadu at that time. A year later, a Sri Lankan intelligence assessment concluded that about 14,000 militants from the 'big five' were trained in India.

These numbers were actually deceptive: not all the militants trained in India were engaged in combat operations in Sri Lanka, because the authorities were restraining not only the nature of the training, but also the supply of arms. For example, by the end of October 1984, the EPRLF had received only around three dozen AKMs, SMGs and pistols, while its leadership believed that the consignments delivered to the other movements were only slightly larger. As a result, the paucity of weapon deliveries created a bottleneck affecting the groups totally depending on Indian support. Militants who had achieved training had to stay longer in Tamil Nadu, waiting to receive a weapon before they could be shipped back in Sri Lanka. Despite all these shortcomings and ambiguities, there is no doubt that the Indian support triggered by the Black July riots drastically changed the face

Table 6: Training Camps for Tamil Militants in Tamil Nadu, early 1986

Group	Number of Camps	Number of Trainees
PLOTE	18	2,330
EPRLF	7	73
LTTE	6	495
TELO	5	233
EROS	2	8
TEA	2	31
TELA	4	127
TENA	1	25
RELO	1	13
NLFT	1	2
ECPR	1	4
TMPP	1	6

of the Sri Lankan conflict. This is why 1983 is considered as the year when the 'First Eelam War' began.[51]

The Calm Before the Storm

It took several months for the synergy between the influx of volunteers, training in India, and the arms deliveries to became obvious in northern Sri Lanka. On the contrary, the late 1983 and early 1984 there was a period of lulls in attacks, during which the insurgents only ran a few bank robberies for financing purposes, and launched relatively few assassinations of informants. Indeed, during this period several of the groups gained notoriety for 'setting examples' with their treatment of 'traitors' and 'anti-social elements'. For example, in early 1984, the LTTE launched the campaign of 'lamp post killings': five individuals were tied to phone polls and executed with one shot in the head. A sixth person was beheaded and a notice explaining that the victim was a traitor left near the body.

Subsequently, the insurgents began deploying mines as their principal weapon. This campaign began on 11 August 1984, when six soldiers, underway in a jeep, were killed near Mannar. On 2 September, four police commandos were killed, and 10 wounded, in Point Pedro. On 19 November, even the Northern Security Forces Commander, Colonel A. Ariyapperuma, was killed by a landmine near Jaffna. At first, the new threat proved relatively easy to cope with, as the presence of a mine being buried in the road was usually betrayed by a patch of freshly removed soil. However, the insurgents soon learned to avoid this by digging tunnels under the road to place their devices, thus making them much more difficult to detect. Furthermore, the deadliness of the mines was enhanced by the fact that many were remote-controlled, and could be detonated at the most effective moment. Soon enough, army troops had to advance on foot in front of their vehicles to inspect the roads.

A mortar crew from the TELO undergoing training in India. (TELO via Adrien Fontanellaz)

A TELO militant with a 60mm portable mortar, during training in one of that group's camps in India. (TELO via Adrien Fontanellaz)

Usually, the mines were home-made by the insurgents and weighted between 50 to 75 kilos. Their sophistication grew considerably over the time. For example, when the SLA reacted by purchasing so-called Mine-Resistant, Ambush-Protected Vehicles (MRAPs) from South Africa, which had an inducted V-shaped hull, the PLOTE developed the BCM-85 designed specifically to be hung in a tree, with the force of explosion orientated downward.

Mines were not the only result of the insurgent's ingenuity and technical resourcefulness, which was often necessary to compensate for the Indian refusal to deliver specific weapon systems, such as mortars. By 1985, the insurgents had begun to use crude, home-made mortars with around half a kilometre range to harass security forces positions. The first attempts to develop home-made mortars had been made by a small team of the EPRLF, led by a young graduate of Peradeniya University. Starting from a blank sheet, but with the help of military literature, they experimented with several prototypes for months. At least one of them was killed by a shell that detonated prematurely. Thereafter, the other insurgent groups further refined

Pirabhakaran with the core of his group during training in India, in the mid-1980s. (Rohan Gunaratna)

these early designs. The LTTE noticeably developed several models ranging from 50mm to 155mm. The shells were propelled by black powder instead of nitrocellulose, and their charge was detonated either by contact fuses or time fuses. The tubes were cast in aluminium or iron and all these weapons were accordingly short-ranged. The LTTE's 155mm cast-iron tube "Kutty Sri" mortar could lob a shell over a range of 1,500 metres. These homemade mortars and their ammunition had the advantage of being very cheap to produce too, with a cost of LKR200 for a shell containing 5kg of explosives.[52]

CHAPTER 5
OPPOSING FORCES – THE BIG FIVE

Although they had many similarities and shared a common goal, the major insurgent movements evolved differently over the time: partially because their strategies varied, but also because they did not have the same resources. Hence, when, from around mid-1984 on, the hostilities escalated again, the militant movements did not follow the same modus operandi nor played the same part. Nonetheless, the insurgent attacks became ever more frequent and involved increasing numbers of fighters until mid-1985, when a brief cease-fire took place.

Tamil Eelam Liberation Organisation

The TELO had been devastated in 1981 by the loss of its two main leaders. They were succeeded by Sri Sabaratnam, a native of Jaffna. This group was an exception among the insurgent movements because it kept an essentially nationalist ideology, which might explain why Sabaratnam was perceived as 'favoured by the RAW'. Whatever was the case, the TELO was the first to benefit from Indian training and – also as a result of its more encompassing ideology – also the first to attract a wave of new volunteers. This early quick-start proved decisive and allowed the movement to be the largest among the Big Five by the end of 1984, as well as the military strongest, certainly on par with the LTTE.

The TELO placed the emphasis on rather large-scale and spectacular operations – which were also a good recruiting tool – and the movement attracted several gifted commanders, such as A Gnanasekaran (alias Mizo) or Das, whose reputation was such that the latter was allegedly feared even among LTTE militants. However, this was to prove a rather temporary condition: the group was hopelessly over dependent on the Indian support. Furthermore, the TELO was only loosely centralized and in time became divided into several factions. By 1986, two of these turned against each other, resulting in the Das' murder. The clash weakened the TELO enormously: overnight, it not only lost its best military commander, but also the mass of its experienced fighters as the Das' subordinats defected en masse. Finally, the militants of the TELO were considered – at least in Jaffna – as ill-disciplined and sometimes involved in criminal activities such as robberies or even assassinations. How much the latter was really the case remains unclear: it is certain only that multiple militant groups of this period are known to have conducted robberies and then accused somebody else of their deeds.

After keeping a low profile for most of 1984, the TELO became responsible of several of the most daring operation run by the militants. At 1430 hrs on 20 November 1984, at least 35 militants wearing SLA uniforms took positions near the Chavakachcheri police station, then occupied by 75 policemen, including several police commandos. They

Sri Sabaratnam, leader of the TELO. (TELO via Adrien Fontanellaz)

A Gnanasekaran (alias Mizo) was one of best military commanders of the TELO. (TELO via Adrien Fontanellaz)

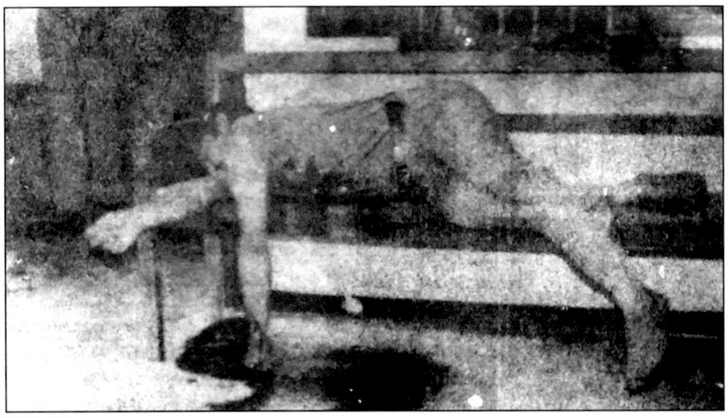

The body of one of 24 police officers killed during the LTTE's attack on the police station in Chavakachcheri on 20 November 1984. (Albert Grandolini Collection)

lured the sentries into opening the facility's main gates by dispatching a young boy who pretended he wanted to replace a lost ID card, and immediately assaulted the station.

However, this assault was conducted to cover other militants that parked a truck loaded with several tonnes of explosives right next to the police station. Once the truck was in place, the driver signalled the imminent explosion with a whistle and the attack party withdrew. The detonation of the charge devastated the station and one of its two-storey buildings collapsed. In the following minutes, schoolboys swiftly searched the rubble to retrieve weapons and give them to the militants. The whole operation lasted around 15 minutes and killed 24 policemen and three civilians. As the beleaguered police officers had alerted the nearby SLA garrison, they dispatched reinforcements, but this move had been expected: another group of the TELO set up a carefully laid ambush along the road at Kaithady. Army troops suffered several casualties when the ambush was triggered by a landmine detonation, and the militants thus gained the necessary time to withdraw safely.[53]

Yal Devi attack

The next major TELO operation took place the 19 January 1985, at night, and targeted the Yal Devi train along the Colombo-Jaffna railway – one of the most important transportation facilities on Sri Lanka. Near Murulandy, around 70 kilometres from Jaffna, and while travelling toward Colombo, the train was derailed by the detonation of nine out of chain of 12 mines buried in the roadbed, around 2030 hrs. Each of the mines weighed around 100 kilos, with charges made out of gelignite, and as a result, eleven cars were completely destroyed. The insurgents had also forewarned the Tamil population and the train was largely unoccupied that day: thus, the number of civilian casualties was reduced to 12, instead of the hundreds who would have died if the train had been full as usual. Strikingly, this did not entice the army – which was in charge of the train protection – to take additional security measures. Thus, the Yal Devi only carried the usual platoon-sized escort from the 1st SLLI, on that ocasion under lieutenant Angelo Peiris. Nevertheless, the insurgents claimed to have killed as many as 298 soldiers – more than tenfold than the army actually suffered: 26 KIA. Nevertheless, after this attack, the railway traffic between Jaffna and Central Sri-Lanka was concluded as too risky by the authorities, and stopped altogether.

On 9 May 1985, TELO took the army head-on and launched a large-scale assault against the Camp Kokavil. Defended by a detachment from the 1st SLLI, this had been on the receiving end of an attack three months earlier. Thus, it was well-protected, including an extensive minefield around its perimeter. To overcome this obstacle, the insurgents stole two bulldozers, and made them bullet proof by wielding on armour plates. Although the TELO later claimed to have killed 48 troops, this attack was actually repulsed by the 1st SLLI, which suffered only 1 KIA that day. Indeed, even if the two bulldozers might have successfully breached the defence perimeter, they were stopped cold by a few RPG rockets fired by the defenders (ironically: RPG-7s had just entered service with the SLA). On the contrary, nine TELO fighters were killed during the assault, including Mizo, their commander, who had been involved in both the Chavakachcheri police station and the Yal Devi operations.[54]

Eelam Revolutionary Organization

By 1983, and although several of its militants had received training from the PLO, EROS had confined its actions in the Jaffna Peninsula to political work. The group was led by a triumvirate which included Ratna, Shankar, and Velupillai Balakumar, a former Bank Manager. Emphasis was placed on the gradual build-up of popular support among the Tamil population, with military actions coming as a second thought, especially as EROS saw actions against security forces as counter-productive – due to the reprisals these triggered against the Tamil civilians. Thus, in 1985, an EROS spokesman explained that:

'We do not believe in "hit and run" tactics as the only way to

A map of Sri Lanka, with all major air bases and airfields, military- and naval bases as of mid-1980s. The areas along the western, northern and eastern coast were claimed by the LTTE as 'Tamil Eelam'.

Centrepiece of the RCyAF and the SLAF for all of the 1960s and 1970s were 12 DHC-1 Chipmunk T.Mk 10 basic trainers, acquired in three batches between 1952 and 1953. About a dozen generations of future pilots earned their wings while flying the type before this was withdrawn from service in 1985. For most of that period, Sri Lankan Chipmunks wore the livery illustrated here, consisting of 'high speed silver' finish overall, and the yellow 'trainer band' around the rear fuselage. Serials were re-applied several times, and thus varied in size and form over time. Illustrated in this colour profile is the original shape of national insignia applied on this type, with a sizeable gap between the roundel and its 'wings' on the fuselage. Notably, the roundels applied on top and bottom surfaces of the wing had their 'wings' applied in complete fashion. (Artwork by Tom Cooper)

A total of six DH.104 Doves served as light transports with the RCyAF and then the SLAAF, from 1955 until 1982. All wore civilian-style livery consisting of white on the top of the cabin and fin, a red cheat line and silver-grey on bottom fuselage and the wing. Large title 'Sri Lanka Air Force' was always applied in black, in English on the port side of the cabin roof, and in Sinhalese on the starboard side, while serials were applied in the usual position above the fin flash. As far as is known, for most of their careers, Sri Lankan Doves had the roundels applied on the top surface of the left, and bottom surface of the right wing. (Artwork by Tom Cooper)

The Beechcraft Super E 18S was the civilian variant of a twin-engined trainer and utility aircraft from the late 1930s, better known for its military variants like the AT-11 Kansan or C-45 Expeditor. Production commenced in 1955 and the type saw widespread service in the USA and around the world. One E18S was originally acquired by the Survey Department of the Sri Lankan government, and then taken over by the SLAF. It received the same livery as that applied on Doves, and is known to have been flown for the last time in 1993 – when it was taken over by the Air Force's Museum. (Artwork by Tom Cooper)

BAC Jet Provosts, 12 of which were acquired in 1958-1959 period, were the first jets and the first fighter aircraft of the RCyAF. This example is illustrated as on delivery, painted in 'high speed silver' finish overall. Roundels were applied in six positions (i.e. on top and bottom surfaces of both wings, and on the rear fuselage), together with serial numbers, which were always in black. (Artwork by Tom Cooper)

During the 1970s, ever bigger portions of airframes of SLAF's Jet Provosts were painted in red. Initially, the entire front fuselage was painted in red, and red streaks were applied on wing-tip fuel tanks, as shown here. By the time the last few remaining examples were withdrawn from service in 1982, most of them had their entire fin and the rear fuselage painted in red too. (Artwork by Tom Cooper)

The two C-47s of the SLAF saw intensive service during the 1970s and 1980s, until replaced by HS.748s, and then Y-8s. Both examples wore the usual 'civilian-style' livery in white on the top of the fuselage and the fin, the red cheat line, and silver-grey undersides and wings. Serials were usually applied as illustrated here, but this aircraft was also photographed while wearing its serial applied in a much bigger fashion, and below the fin flash. (Artwork by Tom Cooper)

A reconstruction of the original look of one of five MiG-17s (original variant, without the afterburner) as these looked shortly after their delivery. All were painted with two layers of clear lacquer mixed with 5% of aluminium powder, resulting in colour variously described as 'silver grey' or 'bare metal overall'. National insignia was applied only on the rear fuselage and the fin, and the serial in relatively thick letters and digits atop the fin. (Artwork by Tom Cooper)

During the 1970s, Sir Lankan MiG-17s received big red streaks on their forward fuselage and drop tanks, as well as covers for air-brake actuators painted in red. Serials were re-applied with the help of stencils in thinner fashion. There are indications that during the same period, national markings were applied on the top of the left wing and the underside of the right wing, while serials should have been applied on the top of the right wing and the underside of the left wing. (Artwork by Tom Cooper)

The sole Sri Lankan MiG-15UTI was painted in a similar fashion to the MiG-17s, and received the same kind of red insignia during the 1970s. Notable is that this was an aircraft from earlier production batches, still equipped with slipper-type drop tanks. (Artwork by Tom Cooper)

Sri Lankan Bell 206 Jet Rangers originally wore civilian-style livery in red and white. Following their overhaul and upgrade to 20C configuration, most received a camouflage pattern consisting of glossy dark green overall. The latter tended to wear out due to intensive use, often showing traces of the old colour. Armament – usually consisting of a rocket launcher on the port side, and a gun pod on the starboard side, was installed on a pylon protruding through the doors of the rear cabin. Notable is that the national insignia (applied on both sides of the cabin) was significantly decreased in comparison to earlier times. (Artwork by Tom Cooper)

Most of the SLAF's SF.260TPs were initially camouflaged in two, later three shades of green on top surfaces and sides, and light blue grey on their undersides. Roundels were applied in only two positions (on either side of the rear fuselage), while serials were always applied in black on the fin, though often in letters and digits of different size. While all aircraft were delivered with four underwing hardpoints, only the inboard pair of these seems to have been regularly used – and then primarily for different types of French- and US-made pods for unguided rockets. (Artwork by Tom Cooper)

Dassault Mirage 2000H interceptors – 40 of which were ordered in 1982 – were still a new appearance in the Indian Air Force as of 1987. Deliveries began in 1984, and the type entered service with two premier air warfare units of the IAF, No. 1 and No. 7 Squadrons, over the following two years. For their involvement in Operation Poomalai, six Mirage 2000Hs from No. 7 'Battle Axes' Squadron were re-deployed from their home-base at Gwalior to Yelalanka airfield, from where four flew the escort sortie for An-32s over Sri Lanka in the configuration illustrated here: three drop tanks and a pair of French-made R.550 Magic Mk I air-to-air missiles. As usual for the 1980s, all were painted in *gris bleu moyen clair* (FS26375) on top surfaces and undersides, with a standard camouflage pattern in *gris bleu moyen fonce* (FS25164) on top surfaces and sides, while their radomes were painted in radome black (FS37038). Roundels were applied in six positions, while serials were usually worn on the top of the fin, and near roundels on undersides of each wing. (Artwork by Tom Cooper)

With successive governments assigning only minimal budgets for defence purposes in the 1950s, and there being no obvious threat, the Royal Ceylonese Army was slow to introduce armour. The first armoured vehicles were four FV701 Ferret Mk I scout cars, acquired in 1955, when they entered service with the Reconnaissance Squadron. Although there was an option for installation of a pintle-mounted .30 Browning HMG, they were usually not armed. (Artwork by David Bocquelet)

The RCyA and then the SLA acquired much larger numbers of Ferret Mk IIs: in addition to two examples purchased in 1955, further batches followed in 1971 and 1979, increasing their totals to 36 and then 47. Together with Daimler Armoured Cars, they saw intensive combat service during the insurgency of 1971. In contrast to the lightly protected Ferret Mk I, the Mk II had thicker side and rear hull armour, and a HMG installed inside a three-door turret. As far as is known, all were painted in olive green and wore no other insignia. (Artwork by David Bocquelet)

In 1958, the RCyA acquired 12 Daimler Armoured Cars, enabling it to expand the Reconnaissance Squadron into the Reconnaissance Regiment consisting of two squadrons (each with three troops). While refurbished before delivery, and originally a highly successful design, the Daimlers were old vehicles that proved less successful as internal security vehicles. Their armament consisted of a 40mm 2-Pdr cannon and a coaxially-installed 7.92mm Besa machine gun. Like Ferrets, RCyA's Daimlers were painted in olive green overall and wore no other insignia. (Artwork by David Bocquelet)

The SLA purchased around 40 Alvis FV601 Saladin armoured cars during the 1980s, of which around two dozen were usually operational with the 1st Reconnaissance Regiment. The type saw extensive service in the fire-support role, but proved too thinly armoured for the threat. All the vehicles of that period were still painted in olive green overall. (Artwork by David Bocquelet)

The SLA obtained a total of 67 Alvis FV603 Saracen APCs starting in 1984. The type saw intensive deployment during the civil war, when deployed in small detachments, usually consisting of two Saracens and one Saladin. During the first few years of their service Sri Lankan Saracens retained their olive green overall livery, and their primary armament consisting of one Browning M1919 machine gun. (Artwork by David Bocquelet)

The SLA received a batch of BTR-152 APCs from the former USSR in 1971, however the type proved unpopular in service, primarily due to the lack of technical documentation in the English language, and the Soviet refusal to deploy necessary advisors. As far as is known, all the vehicles in question were painted olive green overall. (Artwork by David Bocquelet)

A beautiful study of the first Jet Provost manufactured for Sri Lanka, taken before delivery. Visible to advantage is the form of national markings and position of serials applied on undersurfaces of the wing. (BAe Herritage)

One of five MiG-17s of the SLAF, delivered from the Soviet Union in April 1971 – as seen in the late 1970s, after receiving prominent red flashes along their forward fuselage, by when most of the fleet was in storage. (John Fricker Collection, via Simon Watson)

Availability of SF.260TPs provided the SLAF with a significant increase in fire-power, and their presence was heavily felt by insurgents during Operation Liberation. While most of the fleet received a camouflage pattern consisting of two or three shades of green-grey colour, this example used to serve as SIAI-Marchetti's demonstrator, and was rushed into combat wearing an unusual desert-style camouflage pattern. (Milpix/Martin Hornliman Collection)

Protest of a group of Tamil Students, members of the TELO branch in Madras, on 1 February 1985. (Albert Grandolini Collection)

By 1984, heavily armed TELO militants became a common sight on the streets of various towns in northern Sri Lanka. (Albert Grandolini Collection)

While they were still allies (from left to right): Leader of the TELO, Sri Sabaratnam, Prabhakaran from the LTTE, Balakumar from the EROS, and Padmanabha, from the EPRLF. (Adrien Fontanellaz Collection)

Leaders of the Tamil insurgency with Indian politicians. From left to right, Pathmanabha (EPRLF), Sabaratnam (TELO), Tamil Nadu Chief Minister Marudur Gopalan Ramachandran, Balakumar (EROS), , and Premachandram (EPRLF), in early 1980s. (Rohan Gunaratna)

mobilise the people. In fact, instead of mobilising and organising the people it has demobilised them. This is the bitter experience that draws from the state of our revolutionary struggle for Liberation. We, too, believe that means justify the end. But the end should be the people and not the institutions or organisations or military operations. Our aim should therefore be to carry out military actions which should act as agents to mobilise people, disperse the enemy, not allowing the enemy to concentrate its forces in one area [...].Our military strategy should be to cause striking blow to the economy of the enemy and to bring about a psychological set back to armed forces. In essence our political and military tactics should be subversion and sabotage.'[55]

Correspondingly, EROS rarely launched attacks against security forces, although by 1985 it had enough military capabilities to defeat a police operation targeting one of its camps. According to the movement, on 3 April 1985, a platoon-sized detachment of the Special Task Force, tipped off by local informants, advanced toward an EROS camp in the area of Batticaloa, but was forced to retreat after having being ambushed by the militants, who did not suffer any casualties in return.

Overall, deliberate attacks such as an ambush against another police patrol in the Amparai district on 25 April 1985 remained the exception rather than the rule. Indeed, EROS's trademark became its bomb attacks. On 28 June 1984, a bomb exploded in the Oberoi Hotel in Colombo and killed a female employee. The device was probably intended to target Israeli advisors which were staying in the same hotel at that time. A few months thereafter, the EROS conducted a blitz against the capital. On 8 October, three bombs damaged a pipeline connecting the harbour and the Sapugaskande oil refinery while, on 22 October, at least nine bombs exploded in the capital in several locations, including the vicinities of the Fort Railway Station, the Home Ministry Office and TV stations. The attacks killed three persons and triggered a wave of panic, especially as the bombs all exploded within less than three hours.

On 10 April 1985, the EROS initiated what it called the 'Spring Campaign' by detonating a bomb in the train station adjacent to Katunayake IAP, on the eve of the arrival of British Prime Minister Margaret Thatcher in Sri Lanka for an official visit. On 30 April, another bomb exploded near the Sri Lanka Army Headquarters in Colombo, although causing only limited damage. On 9 May 1983, EROS operators killed four policemen in the vicinity of Trincomalee with a massive bomb. The main objective of the operation was to scare away visitors from Trincomalee, which had continued to attract tourists in large numbers.

A much larger operation took place ten days later, when EROS guerrillas invested a base camp of expatriates' employees of a US consortium working on a large-size irrigation scheme in the Polonnaruwa region. The 122 American and Europeans workers and their families were expelled from the site, which was then thoroughly destroyed by the insurgents. Meanwhile, another party seized a nearby security post on the A1 road to block any arrival of reinforcements, killing several security forces personnel in the process. On 11 July

1985, one EROS militant was captured by the Police in Colombo. Suspicious policemen had investigated his van and found inside a time-bomb with 120 kilos of Gelignite, which EROS operatives planned to use to assassinate President J.R Jayewardene.

EROS' bomb attacks continued thereafter and became bloodier, although the identity of the authors of the bombing of an Air Lanka Lockheed TriStar, in early May 1986, prior its take-off from Katunayake toward the Maldives Islands, and which killed 16 passengers and wounded another 41, remains controversial. On the other hand, EROS did claim another bomb attack on 7 May against the Central Telegraph Office in Colombo, which killed 14 people. A cement factory in Trincomalee, and a bottling factory in Colombo were also bombed by EROS on 21 and 30 May 1986, respectively. In the first case, the insurgents had forewarned the workers to evacuate the site, but eight people died and another 50 wounded in the second case. Despite its widely different strategy, EROS was the only group which maintained good relationships with the LTTE and was considered as reliable by the later leadership.[56]

A still from a video showing a typical insurgent camp (in this case one of the TELO) in the Vanni area in the 1986-1987 period. (Adrien Fontanellaz Collection)

PLOTE's Self-Destruction

By July 1983, PLOTE had been weakened by several raids by the security forces. However, the group remained well-funded, thanks to a series of bank robberies. On 23 September 1983, the PLOTE made a tremendous propaganda coup by organising and supporting a massive jailbreak of arrested Tamil militants detained in the Batticaloa prison.[57]

Putting to good use the training opportunities which followed Black July, the movement grew massively, with various assessments ranging at between 5,000 and 8,000 members. The PLOTE camps were organised in platoons, divided into sections, and while the training provided to its militants did not differ from other groups, it introduced the middle-eastern practice of 'walking through fire' demonstrations – which cost the life of a few militants in various accidents. Furthermore, it established links with the Palestinian PFLP which provided training to a small number of its activists. It also had its own radio station, the Voice of Thamileelam which broadcasted in Tamil and Sinhalese languages. Its ideology remained Marxist-orientated and, as with EROS and EPRLF, it claimed that its strategy followed the Maoist pattern emphasizing the building of a popular base.

However, this was the theory rather than the reality. The bulk of the militants were kept in their camps in Tamil Nadu where they constituted a 'force in being'. Indeed, the PLOTE operations were not on par with its apparent strength. Its most notorious action in 1984 was launched on 21 October, in form of an attack on the Killinochchi Court, where the militants seized 72 shotguns and Lee Enfield .303 Rifles. Another major action was launched on 25 April 1985, in the form of an attack against a police station mere 60 kilometres from Colombo, were the militants killed a police officer and seized a stock of weapons. Approximately one year later, between June and July 1986, the PLOTE had escalated the tempo of its operations, but these remained mostly small-sized ambushes or attacks in locations such as Mannar, Vasivilan, Mullaitivu or Point Pedro.

Meanwhile, militants in the Tamil Nadu camps were increasingly complaining about their monotonous life, while the movement encountered additional problems. PLOTE's leader, Uma Maheshwaran turned increasingly authoritarian while lacking in diplomatic skills. Eventually, his actions were to prove devastating for the group. By 1984, he not only had fallen out of favour with Marudur Gopalan Ramachandran, the powerful Tamil Nadu political leader, but also with the RAW – especially because one of the movement's publications began to denounce past Indian Army actions in Bangladesh in 1971. In turn, the Indians drastically reduced their support, leaving the movement able to arm only a fraction of its combatants. Eventually, the movement was left without a choice but to turn toward other suppliers and, by early 1985, had negotiated a contract worth $300,000US with a Taiwanese arms dealer for the delivery of a large shipment, including 1,400 rifles, 300 Sten sub-machine guns, and six long-range radio sets. However, Indian customs seized the consignment after its arrival in the port of Madras and, despite PLOTE's leadership's pleas, New Delhi turned down all the requests to relinquish it: in this fashion, all the Tamil insurgent groups were 'reminded' of the fact that antagonising their benefactors would result with severe consequences.

PLOTE's bad fortunes continued thereafter: the group not only lost a large amount of money while trying to secure a second large arms shipment (the Palestinian middleman simply disappeared), but its failures further aggravated tensions within its ranks, eventually triggering a series of purges. Dozens of militants were tortured and summarily executed: sometimes dumped into burning oil cauldrons in front of their comrades, to 'serve as example'. Others were sent back to Sri Lanka, only to be executed on boats and their bodies thrown into the Palk Strait. Ultimately, such treatment resulted in mass defections: by 1986, the PLOTE had ceased to be a major factor within the insurgency. Its final actions included involvement in a coup attempt on the Maldives, in 1988, while Uma Maheshwaran was assassinated in Colombo in 1989, by gunmen of his own moment.[58]

The EPRLF

Until 1983, the EPRLF – exactly like the EROS – had concentrated on political work and had remained utterly devoid of revenues (to the point that its leadership, staying in Tamil Nadu, sometimes survived on the brink of starvation, lacking the means even to buy tickets for public transport). The influx of volunteers which followed Black July had an adverse effect on the rigorous self-discipline which characterized its militants until then, as explained by one of the members of the group initial core:

'We never lost track of the essential questions: Why should we fight? Who are our enemies? Who are our friends? How do we interact with other groups? But the massive rush to join Tamil groups destroyed our desire to train the boys politically. When we insisted on the importance of politics and ideology, many of the new recruits threatened to leave us. Some actually left us.'[59]

Nevertheless, the EPRLF emphasis remained on political and organisational work, with military operations coming as a lesser overall priority – even if Kandasamy Pathmanabha, the Secretary General of the movement, had benefited from military training in Lebanon. Its armed wing, the PLA, did launch some operations from time to time. The first of these, which made the movement famous abroad, proved to be a blunder. On 10 May 1984, PLA kidnapped a couple of American expatriates, working for a US-funded development project, from their house in Jaffna. PLA than made known that 20 Tamil prisoners were to be released and LKR50 million in gold paid to free the two hostages. As the payment of the ransom was to take place in Tamil Nadu, the operation deeply embarrassed the Indian authorities which applied tremendous pressure upon the leadership of the EPRLF – including threats by the RAW to cut any support to them. Both US hostages were released on 15 May 1984.

One year later, on 4 May 1985, PLA was the first insurgent group to use armoured bulldozers. Deploying one of the machines, supported by homemade mortars, its fighters attacked the Naval Base Kankesanthurai while launching diversionary attacks in Jaffna. They also took the precaution to mine the 18 kilometre road connecting Jaffna to the base, and thus prevent the arrival of reinforcements. However, after a five hour long battle, the insurgents had to withdraw.

Training of the 6th Group of LTTE's militants at the camp outside Kulathur, in India, in 1985-1986. (Photo by Wasanthan/LTTE, via Rohan Gunaratna)

One of LTTE's home-made mortars, as seen in 1986. (Adrien Fontanellaz Collection)

A still from a video showing a production of a mortar bomb in one of LTTE's 'cottage workshops'. (Adrien Fontanellaz Collection)

In their wake, they left between 20 and 30 of their number, including one woman (the EPRLF was the first Tamil insurgent group to enlist women for combat service). A few months later, on 5 February 1986, the PLA launched another attack against the Point Pedro army camp, but was beaten back again, suffering seven casualties. The movement did better in keeping its edge in mortar technology: by 1986, it was producing designs with calibres of 90mm and 120mm, and a range of 3,000 metres; superior to anything other groups could offer.[60]

Breeding the Tigers

By mid-1983, the LTTE was the best-organised and the most active of all Tamil militant groups. However, the Tigers deliberately chose to expand much slower than the other groups and, as a result both TELO and PLOTE outnumbered them by the end of 1983. As of early 1986, LTTE was estimated to include between 1,500 and 2,000 militants – as well as several hundred active sympathizers, more or less waiting to be integrated in its ranks.

Indeed, and despite the influx of volunteers willing to join the insurgents, Velupillai Pirabhakaran refused to lower the exacting recruitment standards in his movement, or alleviate its disciplinarian nature, which remained more severe among the Tigers that in the other movements. Orders were to be followed without any discussion and to the letter, and accusations of dereliction of duty could have deadly consequences. For example, two militants – one male and one female – are known to have been executed in the late 1980s, when it was discovered that they had sexual intercourse while on guard duty. Hence, potential candidates continued to be carefully selected before being submitted to a several-months long probation period in the course of which they were tasked with missions such as spying, propaganda work, or acting as messengers. Indeed, the movement always placed a great emphasis on using well-trained fighters, as expressed by its leader during the mid-1980s:

> With just 50 people I can do a good job, instead to have a bloated but useless 500.[61]

It is only after having proven their worth during these tests that the candidates were formally allowed in the movement. This integration was marked by a ceremony during which they had sworn allegiance to the LTTE and his leader by pronouncing the following vow:

> I swear to sacrifice my life to achieve the main ambition of our revolutionary movement, of forming Tamil Eelam. I promise to follow all orders of our leader Velupillai Pirabhakaran and be loyal

and true to him forever, as I declare my readiness to start training from today. Tiger's thirst is Tamil Eelam.[62]

By 1984, basic military training had been standardized and recruits went through a three-months-long boot camp, followed by another three months of advanced training – as explained by Adele Balasingham, propagandist and wife of Anton Balasingham, who described the courses followed by female recruits in the mid-eighties:

… the training programme begins with a basic three months course followed by an additional advance training period of three months […]. The basic three months training course is rigorous, wide-ranging and a testing ground for the cadres. It is a new experience and makes great demands on their energies and endurance. The day begins at 4-30 a.m. and continues till late evening. The training programme consists of rigorous physical exercises – long distance running, crawling under barbed wires, rope climbing, military parade etc. – along with theoretical and practical exercises on weapons. At the same time, sentry positions in the camps have to be staffed day and night, the cleanliness of the camp maintained etc. Political studies are also included in the training programme.

Following the completion of the three months training programme, and an evaluation of progress, the trainees moved onto the advanced training programme for a further period of three months. During this programme the cadres studied a wider range of heavy weapons more deeply, and were given training in how to handle them. Simulated combat situations with live ammunition were repeatedly undertaken, not only to teach cadres various fighting tactics, but to familiarise them with the sounds and impact of live ammunition.[63]

Three 'Tigers' proudly showing their kuppis – capsules with cyanide that they wore around their necks – enabling them to commit suicide rather than be captured by Sri Lankan security services. (Albert Grandolini Collection)

Ponnaman (alias Kugan, alias Atputhan), was the commander of LTTE's training camps in India in the period 1983-1986. For this photo, he posed in a uniform sourced from Great Britain. (Rohan Gunaratna)

Whenever possible, freshly graduated recruits were gradually engaged in combat activities under the tutelage of already experienced fighters. The most promising militants were identified and then carefully selected to form new cadres. Generally, would-be leaders had to prove themselves in combat and, when in position of command, to lead their men from the front.

From 1984 on, the new members received during their introduction the 'kuppi', a capsule containing cyanide, that they wore around their neck, thus institutionalising the "death rather than surrender" ethos of characters such as Seelan, whose example was to be followed by the other Tigers if and when necessary. Actually, wearing cyanide in order to commit suicide was expressed as a way, for a militant, to opt for a quick and comparatively painless way out, instead of being tortured at length before dying anyway. However, it also symbolized the level of commitment expected from them, and actually contributed to the LTTE's fighters' prestige, as expressed by a 15 years old Tamil girl in 1985, who later became a Tiger herself:

I admired the Tigers the most. They were considered the most successful group in the battlefront. The black thread around their necks that carried the cyanide capsule ('Kuppi') gave them added prestige.[64]

The universal wearing of cyanide phials also revealed another major aspect of the LTTE; the emphasis placed on secrecy. Hence, even if its militants were rarely taken alive, the organisation as whole was

The eventual assassin of Indian Prime Minister Rajiv Ghandi, Thenuli (alias Dhanu), underwent military training with the 7th Group of LTTE's female militants in India. This photograph shows her carrying the LTTE's flag during the graduation ceremony. (Rohan Gunaratna)

Pirabhakan with his bodyguards during training in India in 1985. (Rohan Gunaratna)

functioning on a "need to know" basis, in order to limit the potential damage of an intelligence leak. For the same reasons, the LTTE was the only movement who provided false identities to the Indians, who requested their trainees to give their picture of them as well as their names. Furthermore, while the use of aliases was common to all militant groups, it was strictly enforced in the LTTE, which also forbid any of its militants to even ask about the real identity of comrades, with dreadful consequences in case of infraction. Similarly, militants allowed to leave the movement, something that remained relatively common until the early 1990s, were sworn to secrecy and forbidden to join another movement or engage in political activities thereafter.[65]

Ghost Fleet

From the perspective of the LTTE, the Indian support was a mixed blessing because it also beefed-up other militant groups – and thus, potential rivals – which were hardly active by then. On the other hand, the LTTE benefited from the same advantage as provided to other movements, but its leadership became almost immediately suspicious about New Delhi: they understood that the Indians were willing to use militants as a means of leverage, but would not support the creation of an independent Tamil Eelam, which was LTTE's core – and non-negotiable objective. Correspondingly, Velupillai Pirabhakaran decided to not overtly antagonise the Indians and make the most of their support but, on the other hand, to develop in utmost secrecy the means to continue its struggle independently and without their support if needed.

The Year 1984 began under very favourable auspices for the LTTE. Marudur Gopalan Ramachandran, the aging but powerful Tamil Nadu Chief Minister, began to favour the Tigers and entered a close friendship with their leader. In early 1984, he donated a staggering 20 million rupees to the LTTE, which found itself literally flushed with money. A large part of this sum was invested into developing a maritime shipping capability which would allow the movement to procure its weapons independently, as well as earning further income by transporting legal cargo. This task was given to Vaithilingam Smalingam (alias Shankar) and Tharmalingam Shanmugam (alias Kumaran Padmanabhan or K.P). With the help of a Sri Lankan Tamil merchant navy captain, they created several front maritime companies such as Arasu Maritime Private Ltd. They also bought the Sun-Hing, an old Chinese merchantman, re-named MV *Cholan*, registered in Panama in October 1984. MV *Cholan* was the first of several small merchant that constituted the LTTE's hidden merchant fleet.[66]

To man this naval branch, known as the Sea Pigeons, the LTTE could draw upon the Jaffna Peninsula population, where numerous Tamils had seafaring experience from previous employment on merchantmen or as fishermen. A few years later, the LTTE was operating simultaneously as many as a dozen ships of this kind – all under the supervision of K.P, who answered directly to Pirabhakaran – and had spun a complex web of global reach, allowing him to supply the goods vital for the movement.

In the mid-1980s, the LTTE also began to acquire its own fast-boats. They usually had 15 to 20 feet long hulls made of fibre-glass and were equipped with three 80hp outboard motors (OBM), and were thus very fast on the water, and were used to carry fighters and equipment between the Tamil Nadu and Northern Sri Lanka. This small fleet was to form the basis of the Sea Tigers branch of the movement. From 1986 on, weapons and ammunition worth US$4 million were bought every year from a galaxy of arms dealers. In the meantime, the movement opened offices in virtually every country where a significant Tamil community was present. Over time, funds from the diaspora would become LTTE's main source of income, especially so since 1987, when it became the last significant Tamil armed movement left. Furthermore, the movement also organised a dedicated wing which levied a variety of taxes on the Tamil populations in Sri Lanka proper.

Organising the Tigers

By the end of 1984, the first shipment of weapons, ammunition and explosives – procured in Lebanon, and brought by the Sea Pigeons – had been delivered. Thanks to this infrastructure, the LTTE soon became the better-armed group among the Big Five, but also obtained weapons which the Indians refused to provide. For instance, if the RAW had agreed to train 10 Tigers during six months in the skill of anti-aircraft gunnery, it subsequently refused to provide the corresponding weapons. The LTTE gunners nonetheless soon had the opportunity to put their training to good use thanks to 12.7mm HMGs bought directly from other sources. Perhaps more importantly, this infrastructure allowed the movement to buy modern communications equipment, from long-range HF radio sets to cheap Japanese-made VHF walkie-talkies. With these, the LTTE was able to command, coordinate and control its forces much more effectively than any other groups. Indeed, leaders from other Tamil groups even had to ask the Tigers to let them use the radio equipment in the latter HQ in Madras to let them communicate with their own militants operating in Sri Lanka.

The same year, the movement created an intelligence wing, under Shanmuganthan Sivasankaran (alias Pottu Amman), which later became known as the Tiger Organisation Security Intelligence Service (TOSIS), while all Tamil Nadu training facilities were overseen by a Training Wing under Ponnaman. In 1985, the first three training camps were also operational in the Jaffna Peninsula and in the Wanni, where up to around 400 could be trained at the same time. Another training facility was opened in the east, too. By mid-August 1984, the first female militant began to receive military training, although women were not engaged in combat operations until 1986.

Velupillai Pirabhakaran continued to lead the movement from India, where he stayed until January 1987, and was seconded by Mahattaya, his deputy. In Sri Lanka, the Tigers were organised in a military and a political wing, with similar structures. The difference between the two wings was theoretical to a certain extent, because militants attached to the political wing had often followed military training as well, and could also be mobilised for combat operations. Between 1984 and 1988, Northern and Eastern Sri Lanka was divided between eight regional commanders who were in charge of areas corresponding to the Jaffna, Killinochchi, Mannar, Mullaitivu, Vavuniya, Trincomalee, Batticaloa and Ampara districts. In turn, these regional commanders oversaw the activities of several area commanders who, in turn, were controlling the actions of a varying number of militants. By 1987, the militants of the military wing were organised in 15-man strong sections, and might have been organically divided in two groups of seven fighters, as small-scale ambushes were usually made by either seven-strong or fifteen-strong outfits. Furthermore, for more ambitious operations, area or regional commanders routinely gathered several sections to launch platoon-sized or company-sized attacks. If needed, area commanders could be reinforced by fighters from other areas, or even regions. As already mentioned, the LTTE forces could always rely on support provided by sympathizers, often called "helpers", for logistical or intelligence-gathering purpose.

Although an insurgent force, the movement was also highly bureaucratized. Every single loss and every engagement had to be thoroughly documented and reported to the hierarchy. From time to time, these reports were cross-checked independently by TOSIS to ensure that lower echelons in the hierarchy did not hide any aspects of their actions. In turn, this system allowed the movement to assess the tactics used by even its most isolated units, discard the inefficient leaders and promote those that were providing good results, instead. This association between tight bureaucratic control and an efficient communication network allowed the LTTE leadership to keep control on its fast expanded movement, which was estimated by US intelligence to include 3,000 fighters around September 1986.[67]

Table 7: Major Insurgent Operations against Security Forces, July 1983 – June 1985

Date	Movement	Target
9 Apr 1984	LTTE	Ambush of a SLA convoy
5 Aug 1984	LTTE	Attack on Mullaitivu police station
20 Nov 1984	TELO	Attack on Chavakachcheri police station
19 Jan 1984	TELO	Yal Devi train attack
13 Feb 1984	LTTE	Attack on Army Camp Kokavil
10 Apr 1985	LTTE	Attack on Jaffna police station
4 May 1985	EPRLF	Attack on Kankeesanhurai Naval Base
9 May 1985	TELO	Attack on Army Camp Kokavil

The LTTE was responsible for far more deadly attacks against civilians than any other militant group, but usually did not claim responsibility for them – although some militants did acknowledge some of those in private as 'retaliations against similar atrocities of the security forces'. By the end of 1984, the Tigers had begun to target Sinhalese settlements. On 29 and 30 November 1984 respectively, groups of insurgents invested two settlements in the Weli Oya area, killing 62 people in the first village alone.

A still from a video showing a hotel in the Trincomalee area, blown up by the EROS in 1986. (Adrien Fontanellaz Collection)

Attacks of this kind became recurrent during the following years, as the LTTE intended to expel the Sinhalese from the areas it claimed as part of Tamil Eelam, but also because these indirectly provided them with a military advantage. Even if the government lost no time to organize home guards recruited from the threatened villages, the emerging militias were highly vulnerable when attacked by well-trained and much better-armed Tigers. Thus, the Army had to commit regular troops, dispersed in small detachments, to protect these areas too. Indeed, precious resources were diverted in purely defensive missions, while the LTTE only had to engage small groups of fighters from time to time to keep the pressure on, and hence tie down relatively large numbers of soldiers.

On 14 May 1985, an LTTE commando wearing SLA uniforms, dispatched by Victor – the Mannar regional commander – shocked the whole country by attacking Anuradhapura, a highly symbolic location considered as outside the conflict zone. Having successfully infiltrated the old part of the city aboard a hijacked van, the Tigers disembarked in proximity of the Jaha Sri Maha Bodhi – one of the two most sacred and revered Buddhist sanctuaries in the Island – and then massacred a total of 146 civilians, including several monks, before withdrawing virtually unopposed, despite the presence of no less than three army camps and one air base in the vicinity of the city.[68]

Tiger Claws

The first large-scale LTTE operation after Black July took place on 9 April 1984 in Jaffna town. A group of Tigers ambushed an army convoy commanded by Lieutenant Fazly Lafir, underway in the Hospital Street. As usually, the ambush was opened with the blast of a big mine, and then the insurgents opened fire on the soldiers from the nearby Catholic Church.[69] On 5 August 1984, up to 60 fighters assaulted the Oddusudan police station, in Mannar District, killed two policemen and seized around twenty rifles, but suffered several casualties in the process. In the meantime, the movement announced that it intended to wage a 'sustained guerrilla campaign'.

On 13 February 1985, the Tigers made their first attempt to overrun an army garrison. Their target was Camp Kokavil, garrisoned by the 1st Gajaba Battalion's 30-man strong platoon under Lieutenant Shanta Wijesinghe, and which had been established only days earlier to protect neighbouring Sinhalese settlements. For this operation, the

LTTE concentrated around 100 fighters. The attack began at 0200 hrs in the morning, with a surprise assault intended to simply overrun the camp. However, an alert guard saw insurgents while they were still crawling towards his position, and opened fire initiating a fire-fight – during which the Tigers fired several volleys of RPG-7s – that lasted until dawn, when the insurgents retreated. During the morning, the Army soldiers found 14 bodies of enemy fighters in camouflage fatigues, and were impressed by their equipment, sometimes better than their own. Indeed, they retrieved from the battlefield not only several RPG rounds, but also AKM and M-16 rifles as well as night-vision goggles (NVGs). The LTTE acknowledged the loss of 16 fighters and claimed to have killed 106 SLA soldiers, more than triple the size of the garrison, which had suffered from two soldiers KIA.

Less than two months later, on 11 April 1985, the Tigers launched their largest operation to date, this time in Jaffna town. Up to 200 militants attacked the main Jaffna police station at 2130 hrs, while another group cut the power supply. In a battle that lasted until 0300 hrs the next morning, the LTTE suffered an unknown number of casualties, while destroying two buildings with RPGs and mortar fire, killing four police officers, and claiming to have captured 165 firearms.[70]

SLA troops with the bodies of LTTE militants killed during the attack on one of military camps in 1985. (Albert Grandolini Collection)

An Intractable Conflict

By Mid-1985, the various insurgent groups, with TELO and LTTE foremost among them, had thus-far launched a number of relatively large attacks. However, these were only the most salient militant actions as northern Sri Lanka had become the theatre of much more numerous small-scale incidents which were placing the security forces under a constant strain. Furthermore, by then, the conflict had become endemic in eastern Sri-Lanka too. Even if the insurgents were operating in a less favourable environment in the Trincomalee, Batticaloa and Ampara districts – because the population there was not ethnically homogenous, and thus their power base comparatively smaller – they were able to steadily increase the number of their operations. On 12 May 1985, several soldiers were killed by the insurgents while conducting a cordon and search operation in Karativu, while on 20 May, five policemen died when their jeep was destroyed by a landmine in Kiran, both in Batticaloa district. During the night of 30 May to 1 June 1985, the LTTE launched an attack against the Trincomalee Naval Base, and claimed to have killed several seamen. The Eastern theatre did further tax the Security Forces and prevented them from concentrating on an all-out COIN campaign in the Northern Theatre, and especially in the very heart of the Tamil insurgency; the Jaffna Peninsula.

However, the war was not a one-sided affair and Sri Lankan armed forces repeatedly inflicted telling blows on the insurgents. For the latter, their division into several different groups proved to be both a blessing and a curse. On the one hand, they could not concentrate their forces and follow a coordinated strategy, but on the other hand, successful operations against one movement would not diminish the capabilities of another group, while all of these benefited from secure rear-bases in Tamil Nadu, out of reach of Colombo, where they could reinforce and reorganize themselves at will. In absolute terms, the conflict remained limited, but the situation was rapidly deteriorating; by the end of 1984, the army had lost a total of 28 men KIA, but six months later, this number had grown to 94. The government latter acknowledged that 135 policemen and 115 armed forces personnel had been killed between July 1983 and mid-June 1985. Losses for the security forces for 1985 alone reached 195 men KIA.[71]

CHAPTER 6
OPPOSING FORCES: THE SECURITY FORCES

From 1983 on, the government began to take measure of the threat created by the Tamil insurgents. It became soon obvious that the security forces were not sized nor equipped the face the rising militant groups and accordingly, all the security arms of the State entered into a period of growth and re-equipment. However, since Black July, Colombo could not rely on really significant help from the West to beef up its armed forces. Countries such as the UK were willing to unofficially let private corporations provide some expertise, but were reluctant to supply the necessary arms and ammunitions. The USA, for example, refused to deliver Cobra helicopters, as requested by Colombo. Furthermore, western products came at a price that Sri Lanka could ill-afford. Correspondingly, Sri Lanka turned toward countries such as Israel, Pakistan and China to get what it needed, with the latter two being the only countries willing to provide military assistance. Beijing in particular, via its State-Company NORINCO, was shipping requested equipment very promptly, and these came at unbeatable prices. NORINCO's role was crucial as expressed by Lieutenant General Cyril Ranatunga, head of the Joint Services Special Operations Command (JOSSOP) between 1985 and 1988:

> At a time when all other manufacturing countries of military hardware refused sales and end user licences to Sri Lanka, it must be reiterated that if not for NORINCO, the armed conflict had every reason to end in sheer disaster.[72]

Colombo had also realised the need for better coordination between different armed services. In 1984, a new entity, the Ministry of National Security, was also created and put under the command of Lalith Athulathmudai. Furthermore, a new combined headquarters came into being: the Joint Services Special Operations Command

(JOSSOP), activated on 11 February 1985 to coordinate the security forces operations in Northern and Eastern Sri-Lanka. The armed services were operating under three Security Forces Headquarters covering the areas of the Jaffna Peninsula, the Wanni and Trincomalee respectively. A coordinating Headquarter was also established in Batticaloa, although the area remained primarily under the responsibility of the Police Commandos.

Police Commandos

In early 1983, the Police headquarters had come to the conclusion that it needed a specially trained COIN paramilitary force. A small force of 60 policemen organised in two platoons came into being during the same year, with the support of the Army, which provided training as well as two officers. On 5 May 1984, the new entity was named the Special Task Force (STF), but its men were also known as 'police commandos'. The STF was first deployed in Jaffna to improve the security of police stations. The commandos were better-trained, better-disciplined, and also better-paid than other policemen and established excellent relations with the nearby army units. Unsurprisingly, they soon found themselves on the receiving end of insurgent attacks: on 1 September 1984, one of its trucks blew-up on a remote-controlled landmine between Velvittiturai and Point Pedro. Four commandos were killed and several others wounded, and after these losses the morale of the STF hit rock bottom.

Meanwhile, Ravi Jayewardene, a security advisor and the son of the President, had become one of fiercest supporter of the STF concept. He proved instrumental into contracting the services of the British firm Keeny Meeny Services, which in turn provided ex-SAS instructors to train the STF, with an emphasis placed on COIN and small-units tactics. The police commandos were also re-equipped, replacing their SLR and Lee-Enfield Rifles with M-16s.

The unit expanded massively and in February 1985 took over security duties in Batticaloa district. In April, this area of responsibility was expanded to include the Ampara district. With time, the STF established several small camps which were used as bases to launch COIN, operations usually involving 12 men patrols. While the STF proved ill-suited for operations in the north, where insurgents were growing stronger and stronger and required increasingly heavy firepower to be dealt with, it proved deadly in the east, where militants were still operating in small groups and using hit-and-run tactics. With time, and because of its efficiency and its reputation of ruthlessness, the STF became universally feared by the insurgents.[73]

A Struggling Navy

The role of the Sri Lankan Navy was, meanwhile, critical because its primary duty was to control the maritime accesses to the island, especially the coastline between Mannar, on the western coast, and Mullaitivu, on the eastern coast. Arguably, this was the centre of gravity of the whole conflict because, even if the security forces could inflict heavy blows upon the insurgents in Sri Lanka, these could not be decisive as long as the latter could use Tamil Nadu as rear bases where they could reconstitute their strength at will.

Initially, the SLN was ill-equipped to accomplish this task. The area was navigated by hundreds of fisher boats by day and by night, and thus searching for insurgents was like searching for a needle in a haystack. The situation was further complicated by the proximity of Indian territorial waters, especially so in the Palk Strait. Accordingly, the SLN began acquiring an increasing number of patrol boats from different sources, and bolstered its manpower. By 1986, the latter included 243 officers and 3,072 sailors as well as by 491 men from the Navy Volunteer Force. The Colombo Dockyard Ltd continued to be an

The dense vegetation along the western coast of Sri Lanka proved a true nightmare for the security services – and offered endless hideouts for insurgents. (Photo by Adrien Fontanellaz)

important supplier and built several inshore (IPV) and offshore patrol vessels (OPV), while another local naval builder – Consolidated Marine Engineers Sri Lanka – delivered a small number of 5-tonne IPVs.

The largest vessels built by the Colombo Dockyards were the SLNS *Jayasagera* (hull number P601) and SLNS *Sagarawardene* (P602), delivered in 1983 and 1984 respectively. These two 40 metre-long and 330 tonne heavy ships were not fast, but had good stability, a good autonomy and fairly good accommodations for their 45 crewmembers. Both were armed with two pairs of 25mm guns and two 12.7mm HMGs.

The smaller IPVs had a major problem with their endurance. Naval facilities closest to the Palk Strait were Trincomalee and Colombo: the base in Karainagar near Jaffna was unable to offer the necessary support. Therefore, in 1984 the SLN bought six small merchant vessels, refurbished and modified them to serve as 'surveillance and command ships' equipped with powerful radars. Henceforth, these acted as 'mother vessels' for minor patrol craft. The ships in question became SLNS *Abeetha* (P714), SLNS *Edithara* (P715), SLNS *Wickrema* (P716), SLNS *Mahaweli* (A24), SLNS *Lanka* (A25), and SLNS *Kanthi* (A26).

That year, the SLN also ordered six Israeli Aircraft Industries-made, Dvora Fast Attack Craft (FAC). Ironically, the Israelis were initially reluctant to sell Dvoras, and it took a meeting between Ravi Jayewardene and Shimon Perez to unlock the situation. It's certain that the links between several of the Tamil militant groups and the PLO proved in favour of Sri Lankan demands. These 47 tonne heavy vessels had received hull numbers P453 to P458. Their design proved highly popular in Sri Lankan service and another batch of six followed in 1986 (hull numbers P463 to P468). Subsequent orders ensured that the Israeli designs became the mainstay of the SLN's combat fleet. Three similar, South Korean-built Killer-class boats (hull numbers P473 to P475) completed this force, all of which was subjected to the control of the 4th Fast Attack Flotilla. All Shanghai-II class fast gunboats were controlled by the 3rd Fast Gun Boat Squadron, while all the surveillance ships came under the control of the 7th Surveillance Command Squadron.

In October 1985, the SLN was further reinforced through the acquisition of SLNS *Kandula* (A537) and SLNS *Pabbatha* (A538), two landing ships acquired from Singapore, necessary to ease the supply of land forces. These were followed by fast personnel carriers, SLNS *Hansaya* (A540) and SLNS *Lihiniya* (A541), both commissioned in late 1987.

The SLN also took drastic measures to prevent the enemy from using fishing boats as a cover. On 1 April 1984, a Special Naval Surveillance Zone was implemented along the coasts. Correspondingly, entry into

By 1984, the SLAF operated a total of 6 Cessna 337. Amongst others, these were deployed for maritime patrol duties, foremost over the Polk Strait. At that time, most were still wearing this 'civilian-style' livery applied in the 1970s, but several examples were already armed with machine guns. (SLAF)

the zone, which covered 100 yards from the coast to the sea, was to be announced and approved by police forces. A much more drastic measure was taken in November that year, with a ban on all fishing activities in Northern Sri Lanka. Despite these measures, the growing number of patrol boats, and the use of motherships to support these, the SLN could intercept on average only between one and three insurgent-used boats per month: this was far too insufficient to sever the naval connection between Sri Lanka and Tamil Nadu.

Air-Sea Clashes

At around 2100 hrs of 21 April 1984, an IPV of the SLN detected a suspect speedboat and immediately launched a pursuit. In calm weather, the faster speedboat would have escaped. However, the sea was rough that evening, thus favouring the warship commanded by Lieutenant Somatilleke Disssanayake. As usual, the insurgents were not ready to give up just like that, and they opened fire at their pursuer as they began to approach. The crew of the IPV returned fire but, because Dissanayake's command was armed only with a Bren light machine gun and a few Lee Enfield rifles, the fire-fight lasted more than an hour. By its end, the LTTE speedboat was dead in the water, with most of her crew killed or dying.

Few months later, on 4 August 1984, a similar firefight erupted off Velvittiturai between another patrol boat of the SLN and a LTTE boat. This time, the Tigers lured the sailors by stopping their boat, and then suddenly opened fire at short range, killing at least one sailor before making good their escape.

Before mid-1985, the SLN was only rarely supported by the SLAF. Indeed, the air force was usually able to provide only a single Cessna 337 – based at Palali AB – for maritime patrolling duties. Lacking radar and even night vision goggles, its crew proved unable to operate by night, when most insurgent maritime activities took place. Furthermore, while having a reasonable endurance of five hours, the Cessnas lacked armament. Eventually, the SLAF solved the problem by removing two rear seats to make place for a single airman, armed with a T-56 rifle, to provide at least some fire support. This token capability proved hopelessly insufficient: in practice, pilots tended to dread carrying gunners because these risked shooting the rear propeller.[74] An alternative solution was found in the form of using glass tumblers filled with a Grenade whose safety pins had been removed – as 'bombs of sorts'.

The problem of specialised maritime patrol aircraft continued to trouble the SLAF for decades longer; indeed, until the ultimate defeat of the LTTE. It was only partially solved through introduction of armed helicopters, the actions of which often had devastating results for any speedboats caught in broad daylight, as explained by Tim Smith, a British pilot flying Bell 212s for the SLAF, who recalled a sortie flown in July 1986 as follows:

'As we approached the coast near Mulliyan Namal (the pilot) spotted a fast-boat about half a mile offshore heading west…the crew of the boat had already seen us. One of them was already standing in the back, frantically starting up the other two engines. In no time at all they had all three engines running and were going flat out, heading for the open sea. Namal raced after it and managed to get alongside them fairly quickly. The port side-gunner opened fire as soon as we were in range and was able to put a fairly accurate burst in front of it.

The boat crew realised at once that they weren't going to make it out to sea, and in a racking turn they flung the boat about, heading back for the beach. Caught by surprise, Namal was late in following them round and we overshot the target quite badly. By the time that we had caught up with them again they were fairly close to the beach and closing it fast. With about half a mile to go Namal brought us back alongside again. The cabin filled with the smell of cordite as the side-guns rattled and hammered again. The port gunner put a long burst straight into the boat, hitting the driver hard and toppling him overboard… Back in the boat, the two surviving crew-members had grabbed their weapons and were giving us all they had, bless'em… Rolling out of the turn, we came alongside the boat again and opened fire on it. With 100 meters left to run to the beach, the boat started to burn and seconds later, under a constant stream of fire, it burst into a fireball of red and yellow flame as it ran up onto the beach…'[75]

From Flying Club to a Combat Force

Like all other military services facing the growing insurgency, the SLAF was forced to expand and acquire new capabilities in the face of the threat. Indeed, the air force reacted with a massive expansion program. While the personnel strength was increased from 185 officers and 2,783 other ranks as of 31 December 1983, to 374 officers and 6,232 other ranks on 31 December 1987, a total of nine secondary air bases were overhauled, and seven of these permanently occupied. With several types quickly reaching the end of their service life, the SLAF was forced to launch a major re-equipment program in 1984. An emphasis was placed on the helicopters, which were acquired in unprecedented quantities: a total of 2 Bell 206s, 22 Bell 212s and 8 Bell 412s were introduced to service between 1983 and the end of the decade. Five Jet Rangers were converted from their C18A version to C20B models through modification of the frame and installation of Allison 250-C20B engines, and an increase in fuel capacity. Furthermore, all were armed – usually with a launcher for 2.75 inch unguided rockets on the port side, and a pod for a 12.7mm HMG on the starboard side. This solution was not entirely satisfactory because additional weight put these light helicopters on the verge of their flight envelope: much more satisfactory proved the conversion of Bell 212s by the Singaporean company Heli Orient. The resulting gunships could carry two 12.7mm HMG pods or two launchers for 2.75 Inch unguided rockets – or one of each of these two weapons systems. Two additional machine guns – either two 12.7mm, two 7.62mm, or one of each – were installed on the cabin doors. By 1988, the same helicopters were adapted to carry South African-made Alpha bombs, mounted in tubes fixed inside the cabin.

Lack of experience in the deployment of helicopters for combat purposes prompted the SLAAF to contract Keeny Meeny Services for the necessary expertise. The British company recruited several retired military pilots to act as instructors for the crew of the No. 4 Helicopter Squadron. To the surprise of most of the British involved, the notion of 'instructor' proved slightly more extensive than expected: starting with 1986, they found themselves flying combat sorties.

Another significant step in the history of the SLAF was the search for a replacement for now 35 year-old Chipmunk basic trainers – preferably in the form of aircraft that could be used for light attack too. The Sri Lankans preferred the Brazilian-made Embraer Tucano. However, the president vetoed this choice for cost reasons. The final choice thus fell on the Italian-made SIAI-Marchetti SF.260. Ordered in July 1985, this type was acquired in two variants: 12 piston-engined SF.260WB served as pure trainers with No. 1 Flight Training School, while 11 turbo-prop-powered SF.260TPs served as light strikers with No. 2 Squadron.

The need for such aircraft was meanwhile so urgent that the SLAF leased two SF.260s to be used for conversion training of its pilots, so that these could go into action as soon as the its own aircraft could be delivered. Fifteen pilots from No. 2 Squadron went through an intensive, three month conversion course run with help of an instructor provided by the Italian manufacturer, in the course of which they logged over 300 flight hours. Despite its small size, the SF.260TP aircraft powered by the 420 horse-power Allison 250-B17D turboprop engine could pack a powerful punch on four underwing hardpoints. One of the most common weapons configurations in the SLAF service consisted of two LAU-32/A launchers for seven 2.75 inch unguided rockets and two SIAI pods for 7.62mm machine guns. Later on, the Sri Lankans added locally manufactured GR-50 and SIG-95 bombs to their inventory.

The transport fleet was in need of reinforcements as well. The acquisition of one Beechcraft King Air B200T and two Avro HS.748s in the 1983-1986 period, and six Harbin Y-12s and two Shaanxi Y-8s in 1987, enabled the withdrawal of old and tired DC-3s, Doves, and Herons. The new transports saw extensive service – not only in their original role but as makeshift bombers too. For this purpose, they could be loaded with different models of so-called 'barrel bombs' from the GR series, whose charge (usually made from gasoline and rubber pieces, or from gelignite) was ignited by locally-manufactured AH3 impact fuses (also used in the more sophisticated SIG bombs). The largest of such bombs weighted around one tonne and could be carried only by the two Y-8s. Due to the interruption of the land traffic between central and northern Sri Lanka, transport activities increased dramatically: indeed, by 1985 all the garrisons in the north had to be resupplied by the SLAF and the SLN. As an illustration of the intensively of such operations, it is worth mentioning that while one flight of a Dove per week to Palali was enough in 1983, by 1986 the SLAF was forced to schedule three flights per day with much larger aircraft. During the same period the number of flight hours registered by the SLAF literally exploded: from 5,376.5 in 1983, to 11,887.1 in 1985, and then to 15,041 in 1986.

Despite its expansion in terms of manpower and equipment, the SLAF retained the same order of battle as during the late 1970s: this was centred on the Nos. 1, 2 and 4 Squadrons, dedicated to training, transport and helicopter operations, respectively. Nevertheless, these units began maintaining regular forward-deployed detachments at several of bases closer to the battlefield. On average, one Bell 206 and one Bell 212 were regularly stationed at Palali. They were used not only for liaison and reconnaissance, but also to re-distribute supplies to various smaller army bases. Two other Jet Ranger were usually at Vavuniya and Batticaloa. By 1985, the increasing number of Bell 212s and 412s permitted the replacement of Bell 206s forward deployed at Palali, Vavuniya and Batticaloa.[76]

Table 8: Known Serial numbers of SLAF Aircraft, 1983-1990

Type	Total Number	Serial
Cessna 337	Unknown	CC650, CC652, CC656, CC660
Bell 412	8	CH520, CH521, CH522, CH523, CH524, CH525, CH526, CH527
Bell 212	22	CH535, CH536, CH537, CH538, CH539, CH540, CH541, CH542, CH543, CH544, CH545, CH546, CH547, CH548, CH560, CH561, CH562, CH563, CH564, CH565
Bell 206A/B	9	CH550, CH551, CH552, CH553, CH554, CH555, CH556, CH557, CH558
SA.365C	3	CH531, CH532, CH533
Riley Heron	4	CF803, CR804
DC-3/C-47	2	CR821, CR822
HS.748	3	CR830, CR831, CR832 (re-serialled as CR833 in 1986)
Y-12	2	CR851, CR851
Y-8	6	CR781, CR872, CR873
SF.260TP	11	CT121, CT122, CT123, CT124, CT125, CT126, CT127, CT128, CT129, CT130, CT131
Cessna 150	6	CT150, CT151, CT152, CT153, CT154, CT155
SF.260WB	12	CT160, CT161, CT162, CT163, CT164, CT165, CT166, CT167, CT168, CT169, CT170, CT171

The second HS.748 acquired for the SLAAF was serialled CR830. This photo from the mid-1980s shows it still wearing the civilian-style livery in white, red and silver grey, instead of the camouflage pattern in brown and green, which became common at later times. (Albert Grandolini)

The SLAF acquired 11 SF.260TPs and rushed them to combat operations almost immediately after delivery. (SLAF)

From the mid-1980s, the backbone of the SLAF helicopter fleet were types like (from forward towards the background) Bell 206s, Bell 212s and Bell 414s. These US-made helicopters proved relatively vulnerable to small arms fire and not perfectly suited to the demands. However, they also proved reliable and often proved crucial for the outcome of minor battles. (SLAF)

The two C-47s continued providing faithful services to the SLAF well into the mid-1980s – until they were replaced by Chinese-made Y-8s. Late during its career in Sri Lanka, this example received a much bigger serial on its fin. (SLAF)

Embattled Army

In 1983, the Sri Lankan defence budget totalled US$ 17,463.160. The regular elements of the army included 615 officers and 10,128 other ranks, while the number of volunteers was at 163 officers and 3,293 other ranks. By 1986, the defence budget rocketed to US$39,680,411, and a year later all the way up to US$129,777,471- or 5.54% of the national income. By 1987, the number of regulars had increased to 26,653 (including 1,740 officers) and that of volunteers to 10,772 (including 451 officers). This massive increase of the military – and the Army in particular – taxed the training system heavily. The capacity of the Infantry Training Centre, established on 25 August 1984, was saturated by the intake of recruits that underwent basic training, and the additional necessity to provide refresher training to experienced troops. A dedicated, two-month course became mandatory for all SLA units before their deployment in the north.

The infantry was, and remained, the core branch of the SLA, and its strength was increased. As of 1983, there were four regular and six volunteer battalions. Four additional regular battalions were raised in December 1985, while all existing battalions received an additional fifth company. Another regular battalion was raised in January 1986, while the next wave of new formations followed in 1987, when five infantry battalions (four regular and one volunteer) came into being.

The resulting battalions thus included up to seven companies (including the headquarters and a support-weapons company), and proved rather unwieldy formations, especially in the light of the fact that the SLA lacked experienced battalion commanders. The reaction of Sri Lankans to this experience might appear unusual: they streamlined their companies into four 30-troop strong platoons, divided into three 10-man strong sections each. Each section nominally had nine assault rifles, one light machine gun, and one rocket launcher. The firepower of infantry formations was increased through progressive re-equipment with Chinese-made Type-56-2 rifles, Type-56 light machine guns, and Type-69 rocket launchers (Chinese variants of Soviet-designed AKMs, RPDs, and RPG-7s, respectively).

In addition to expanding its infantry formations, the SLA established a Commando Squadron on 25 March 1980. Commandos were trained in COIN tactics by the British SAS Regiment while others went to India to be trained in airborne operations. One of that squadron's tasks was to protect VIPs and it also kept a detachment in Katunayake IAP for hostage release in case of emergency. The Squadron was expanded and became a regiment six years later, on 15

March 1986.

Furthermore, the SLA experimented with small-sized ad-hoc special forces teams, also with foreign support. In July 1985, 300 men were trained in counter-terrorism skills by a Pakistani training mission led by Brigadier Tariq Mohamed.

A Special Service Group came into being, too, but this experiment did not last. However, another outfit, the Combat Tracking Team, was formed in 1985 around a core of two officers and 38 men, and later evolved into the Army Special Forces. At some point, several infantry battalions included Long Range Reconnaissance Patrol (LRRP) Teams. The concept proved highly successful when a four men team led by Captain Suresh Hashim was infiltrated by boat in the Trincomalee district jungles areas and killed the LTTE district leader in an ambush after a three-day long wait – before it was successfully exfiltrated by a helicopter.

From 1984 on, the Israelis became instrumental in providing the Sri Lankans with specialist skills. In May that year, an Israeli Special Interest Section had opened in Colombo, and soon thereafter, small teams of Shin Bet (Israel's internal security service) operators began training their Sri Lankan counterparts in intelligence techniques.

Furthermore, the SLA was well-versed in jungle fighting but soon concluded that it lacked the necessary know-how in urban combat. Correspondingly, a dedicated course was set at in the Maduru Oya Army Training School in 1986, with the help of a Colonel and

Recruits undergoing basic training at one of the infantry training camps of the Police, in the mid-1980s. Due to continuously increasing demands for additional troops, such facilities grew immensely in importance – and capacity. (Albert Grandolini Collection)

Table 9: Major SLA Infantry Units, 1980-1987

Unit	Abbreviation	Year of Activation
Sri Lanka Light Infantry Regiment		
1st Battalion Sri Lanka Light Infantry	1st SLLI	1950
2nd (Volunteer) Battalion Sri Lanka Light Infantry	2nd (V) SLLI	1950
3rd Battalion Sri Lanka Light Infantry	3rd SLLI	16 Dec 1985
4th Battalion Sri Lanka Light Infantry	4th SLLI	5 May 1987
5th (Volunteer) Battalion Sri Lanka Light Infantry	5th (V) SLLI	15 Aug 1987
Sri Lanka Sinha Regiment		
1st Battalion Sri Lanka Sinha Regiment	1st SLSR	1956
2nd (Volunteer) Battalion Sri Lanka Sinha Regiment	2nd (V) SLSR	1956
3rd (Volunteer) Battalion Sri Lanka Sinha Regiment	3rd (V) SLSR	1969
4th Battalion Sri Lanka Sinha Regiment	4th SLSR	1st Dec 1985
6th Battalion Sri Lanka Sinha Regiment	6th SLSR	10 Aug 1987
Gemunu Watch Regiment		
1st Battalion Gemunu Watch Regiment	1st GW	1962
2nd (Volunteer) Battalion Gemunu Watch Regiment	2nd (V) GW	1964
3rd (Volunteer) Battalion Gemunu Watch Regiment	3rd (V) GW	1965
4th Battalion Gemunu Watch Regiment	4th GW	27 Dec 1985
5th Battalion Gemunu Watch Regiment	5th GW	1 Jun 1987
Rajarata Rifles Regiment		Dissolved 1983
1st Battalion Rajarata Rifles	1st RR	15 Jan 1980
2nd (Volunteer) Battalion Rajarata Rifles	2nd (V) RR	10 Apr 1980
3rd (Volunteer) Battalion Rajarata Rifles	3rd (V) RR	25 May 1980
Vijayabahu Infantry Regiment		dissolved 1983; reactivated 1988
1st Battalion Vijayabahu Infantry Regiment	1st VIR	
Gajaba Regiment		
1st Battalion Gajaba Regiment	1st GR	14 Oct 1983
2nd (Volunteer) Battalion Gajaba Regiment	2nd (V) GR	14 Oct 1983
3rd Battalion Gajaba Regiment	3rd GR	31 Dec 1985
4th Battalion Gajaba Regiment	4th GR	15 Aug 1987

three Captains from the Israeli Defence Force. This course became mandatory for all the infantry company commanders. Greater attention was also placed on intelligence, and the High Command made sure that all the battalions had a functional intelligence group. In the meantime, a Tamil language school was established. By mid-1987, around 300 Security Forces personnel underwent a three month course in this school.[77]

Hotspurs, Saracens, Unicorns and Artillery

In 1980, the Sri Lanka Armoured Corps (SLAC) was expanded through the activation of a volunteer unit, the 2nd (V) SLAC – the troops of which operated in conjunction with the veteran armoured personnel. The Armoured Corps Training Centre was established on 10 January 1984. The fleet of armoured vehicles operated by these units included some 24 Saladins and 36 Ferrets, and was reinforced through the acquisition of Hotspur armoured personnel carriers (APCs) on Land Rover chassis in 1984. Once the latter proved as ill-suited to local circumstances, the SLA bought Saracen APCs and Stalwart amphibious load carrying vehicles to improve the mobility of its armoured squadrons.

The ever-present threat of landmines compelled the SLA to continued purchasing MRAPs of South African design. These included 32 Buffels in 1986. Three years later, the SLA initiated production of its own MRAP, and the Sri Lanka Electrical and Mechanical Engineers developed the prototype named Yakka (or Devil in Sinhalese). In action, the Yakka proved to offer good protection against small-arms fire, but not against land mines. Therefore, further research and development went along the patterns of the Buffel, including a v-shaped hull made of 12.7mm thick armour plates on the front, and 6.3mm armour on the sides of the hull, attached to an Indian-built TATA chassis that was much cheaper than the Mercedes Unimog originals. The resulting design was named Unicorn and produced in several variants: by 1988, 56 Unicorns, 32 Buffels, 10 Hotspurs and 10 Stalwarts were in service.

However, the Sri Lankan Army did not operate its armour on squadron level during the 1980s: instead, each of the SLAC squadrons headquartered in Jaffna, Palali, Killinochchi and Trincomalee was split into troop-sized detachments deployed at different locations. Its troops and vehicles were used for very diverse tasks, ranging from patrol and convoy escort duties (especially along the critical A9 road), to fire-support missions. Typical detachment consisted of one Ferret, one Saladin, and one Saracen. Ironically, the SLA's infantry was not the least enthusiastic about their appearance: armoured vehicles were hard to conceal and attracted enemy fire. Most of the available vehicles were thinly armoured and required infantry protection. In turn, and despite intensive operations, the SLAC casualties were very low: not one vehicle was written off nor did the corps suffer any KIA in period 1983-1985.

Meanwhile, the artillery component was expanded through the addition of two regiments: one volunteer, established in 1980, and one regular, established in 1985. While the original unit continued using guns acquired in the 1970s, the new units were equipped with a miscellany of recently acquired pieces, including vintage, World War II-era, British-made 25-Pounders.[78]

Table 10: SLA Armoured, Artillery, and Commando Units, 1987

Unit	Abbreviation	Year of Activation
1st Regiment Sri Lanka Armoured Corps	1st SLAC	1955
2nd (Volunteer) Regiment Sri Lanka Armoured Corps	2nd (V) SLAC	28 Jan 1980
4th Regiment Sri Lanka Artillery	4th SRLA	
5th (Volunteer) Regiment Sri Lanka Artillery	2nd (V)SRLA	22 Jan 1980
6th Regiment Sri Lanka Artillery	6th SRLA	1 Sep 1985
Commando Squadron		Expanded to a Regiment, 1986

Lack of Long-Term Strategy

Following Black July, the insurgents were busy building-up their strength and thus avoided bigger confrontations with the SLA. Therefore, no ambushes like that of the Four Four Bravo happened, even if the army continued running cordon and search operations, and there was vigorous patrolling activity. The SLA's operations were further impeded by the requirement to help Home Guards to protect Sinhalese settlements against LTTE attacks, but also by the necessity to support the police in the north even in its most basic tasks. Before long, Sri Lankan Army troops found themselves regulating traffic in Jaffna.

Cordon and search operations were run along traditional patterns: soldiers would surround a specific location – usually a village – during the night. Then additional troops would move in to collect all the men between 18 and 35: these would be brought to a pre-determined location and investigated, while other troops would run a house-to-house search, looking for any arms and any other kind of suspicious materials. Virtually any Tamil men that turned up in the wrong place and time, were considered 'insurgents'. A good example of this practice was a cordon and search operation undertaken from 9 until 12 December 1984 in the towns of Jaffna, Killinochchi and Mullaitivu. A curfew was imposed, and then the troops moved in. In three days of raids, they seized a few arms and some ammunition, but also took 700 young men away for interrogation. Initially, such operations proved relatively effective: they regularly resulted in arrests of suspects and seizure of equipment. However, the insurgents quickly learned to post their informants near major military bases and let them monitor military traffic. Because of timely warnings issued by observers, an increasing number of cordon and search operations began turning out no results at all.

The standard 'a jeep and a truck' or 'two trucks' –sized Army patrols proved inefficient too. Not only that the insurgents found such groups easy to ambush, but also easy to avoid. Younger SLA officers developed the first trick that wrong-footed the militants: a few soldiers would jump off such a patrol, and establish an ad-hock checkpoint. Fifteen minutes later, the trucks would return to pick them up, and then repeat the exercise at another location. Such operations were run at random intervals in time and place and thus proved extremely hard for the insurgents to avoid: not only that the absence of military vehicles made such checkpoints hard to detect from sufficient distance, but their short duration prevented any information about their presence to spread.

Another method of SLA operations were night ambushes on

A look down one of the typical dirt roads in the Killinochchi area: such lines of communication offered endless opportunities for ambushes and mining operations by the insurgents – primary reasons for the government's gradual loss of control over northern Sri Lanka in mid-1980s. (Photo by Adrien Fontanellaz)

Most of the armoured vehicles operated by the SLA as of the mid-1980s – such like this Shorland armoured patrol car operated by the SLAF Regiment – proved vulnerable to mines and IEDs deployed by Tamil insurgents in large numbers. (Albert Grandolini Collection)

beachfronts, aimed to intercept some of the insurgent boats. Due to the lack of intelligence, most of these proved fruitless. In one of a very few exceptions, on the night of 23 November 1984, an army ambush party surprised the crew of an insurgent boat shortly after this landed on a beach in the Batticaloa district, killed five, captured 10 AKM rifles and 3,000 rounds of ammunition.

Overall, and despite mixed success, the Sri Lankan military gave as good as it got: while the results were meagre, the LTTE later did acknowledge the loss of 5 militants in 1983, 36 in 1984, and 123 in 1985. Obviously, this was far from being enough to open the prospect of eradicating any of the militant groups. However, much worse was the inherent inability of successive Sri Lankan governments to clearly define a political strategy to end the war. Foremost, the dynamics of the local political scene was such that it made it virtually impossible for Colombo to advocate any solution that would be supported by moderate Tamils. Any such step would be considered 'treachery'. Versa-vice: while the governments of the 1980s did significantly increase the defence budget, they did not think in the longer term. On the contrary, the sole long-term strategy of Colombo was to organize Sinhalese settlements near Tamil majority areas, with the idea that ethnically separated populations would 'somehow get along together with the time'. However, the re-settlement policy played right into the hands of the insurgents who could denounce the related policies as a tool to undermine Tamil communities. Hence, the government lost the opportunity to gain the upper hand in a contest which was anything other than 'lost' – especially because support for militant groups was anything else than universal.[79]

The Dark Side of COIN

The strong presence of the ideology of Sinhalese supremacism among the population and the political class of Sir Lanka had a deleterious effect upon the discipline of the military too. Not only that not all the soldiers involved in the Black July were punished, but the practice of physically assaulting detainees under interrogation was considered 'normal'. Unsurprisingly, the number of cases of outrageous crimes against humanity was continually rising. As many as 272 cases of disappearances of detainees were documented by Amnesty International between June 1983 and April 1986 alone. Indeed, reports about exactions by Sri Lankan armed forces against Tamil civilians first went into hundreds, and then grew even worse after the first massacres of the Sinhalese committed by the LTTE. For example, in the aftermath of the Anuradhapura attack, six men – suspected of being SLN sailors – boarded a civilian ferry off Nainativu Island and murdered 48 civilians. According to Civilian Committees active in the major Tamil towns in the north, retaliation massacres committed by security forces immediately after insurgent attacks occurred on several occasions, such as that on 5 August 1984. That day, after a landmine attack in the vicinity of Velvittiturai, soldiers burnt 130 houses and 90 shops, and opened fire on civilians on several occasions. The STF in particular gained notoriety in this regard, and allegedly routinely burned any village in the vicinity of ambush sites. The police commandos were also suspected of having executed around 40 Tamil civilians arrested in three villages in the Batticaloa area on 16 May 1985. Home Guards militias reportedly also committed exactions against Tamil Civilians.[80]

No doubt, the insurgents operated most of the time in small groups and were usually wearing civilian clothes to blend with the civilian population, and this increased the risks of civilian casualties during firefights. However, the use of barrel bombs by the SLAF was often indiscriminate and had dreadful consequences for innocent civilians. Indeed, due to the gradual loss of control over civilian population, from 1985 onwards, the Sri Lankan military and security services tended to fire at nearly everything suspicious. During cordon and search operations, soldiers became involved in looting valuables from the houses they searched through. Further antagonising were so-called 'incidents of lesser proportions', which occurred regularly. Tim Smith recalled another mission with a Bell 212, from mid-1986:

> We flew over a truck standing at the road junction at Nelliadi a couple of kilometres to the south-west of Point Pedro. As we passed overhead it turned away from us and sped off along the road to Karaveddi in a cloud of dust. Namal swung the "Trooper" around in a blade thumping tight turn and brought the door-gun to bear. He gave a brief order to the gunner, and a stream of 7.62mm machine gun fire raised dust across the road and rattled its way across the cab, shattering the windscreen and killing the passenger. The truck

The predilection of SLAF's gunners to open fire at any truck underway in northern Sri Lanka was reasonably-well substantiated: numerous vehicles were requisitioned and used for transport by the militants, while others mounted heavy machine guns. This is a scene from the training of a Tamil insurgent group in Sri Lanka in 1986. (Albert Grandolini)

> came to a sliding halt in a cloud of dust and steam from the radiator. The driver left the cab at a blind run and almost made it into the coconut groves before the creeping fingers of tracers strolled across his back.[81]

Combined with drastic regulations – like a ban on fishing along the northern coast, and the ban on the use of private cars in Jaffna (only public busses were allowed to circulate for two hours a day) – such actions antagonised the Tamil population ever more. Unsurprisingly, US evaluations of Sri Lankan COIN operations were damning. According to the same, the SLA was suffering from an endemic lack

The acquisition of the first two Shaanxi Y-8s signalled the start of a period in which Sri Lanka began acquiring increasing amounts of Chinese-made armament. This was the first of two aircraft of this type acquired in 1987. (SLAF)

of discipline, widespread corruption, poor training and leadership, and was led by senior officers promoted on the basis of political connections instead of merit.[82]

Certainly enough, the actual situation was even more complex – especially so in the case of the SLA. For example, immediately after the LTTE attack on Anuradhapura, numerous Tamil civilians fearing anti-Tamil riots found refuge inside an army camp near the city. A SLA corporal there went berserk and opened fire at them, instantly killing several. A major who had witnessed the scene reacted by pulling out his pistol and killing the corporal on the spot. Obviously, the damage caused by the undisciplined NCO was already done. Subsequently, the officer was criticised for having shot the corporal outright; on the other side, the incident did not prevent him from ending his career with the rank of a Major-General.

Indeed, many SLA officers were not the least keen to tolerate harassment or mistreatment of civilians. Some went as far as to convince their troops that their misdeeds against the Tamils would unleash upon them the wrath of the gods revered by their victims. Furthermore, many officers understood the problems related to the indiscipline and lack of training, caused by the fast-paced expansion of the army, and a degenerating conflict. Thus, they not only acknowledged, but began addressing such issues too. Eventually, even higher-ranking officers began to change, resulting in a situation where all-encompassing, unfavourable criticism of these was contradicted by examples such as Brigadier-General Denzil Kobbekaduwa, who was re-known for his benevolent, but also extremely demanding, style of leadership.[83]

CHAPTER 7
WAR ESCALATION

The administration of Rajiv Gandhi, appointed Prime Minister following the assassination of his mother, Indira, continued to support the Sri Lankan Tamil insurgents. On the other hand, it also increased pressure, both on the Sri Lankan government and on the Tamil groups, to conduct negotiations and solve the whole conflict by peaceful means. In the meantime, the RAW pressured the 'big five' into creating and adhering to an umbrella organization, which became known as the Eelam National Liberation Front (ENLF), in April 1984. The ENLF included initially the EPRLF, TELO and EROS, and was joined one year later by the LTTE. However, the Indian diplomatic strategy was flawed as it advocated a compromise summarized in the following fashion by Rajiv Gandhi:

> We will not allow an Eelam in Sri Lanka. The maximum we will talk about is the kind of autonomy that is available to states in India.[84]

The essence of such messages was unacceptable for both sides in Sri Lanka: the insurgents were committed to an independent Tamil Eelam, while any kind of a federalist solution was an absolute anathema for most of the Sinhalese. On the other hand, both Colombo and the ENLF were not in a position to ignore New Delhi's wish to organise Peace Talks which had to be held at Thimpu, the capital of Bhutan. During a meeting in Madras between Velupillai Pirabhakaran and RAW officials, the latter made this realty crystal clear: failing to be part of the peace talks would be akin to lose the ability of using the Indian territory as a rear base. Hence, New Delhi, the TULF, the 'big five' and Colombo all sent representatives to Thimpu for a first round of negotiations which began in July 1985 and were followed by a second round in August. Unsurprisingly, the negotiations failed to provide any solution to the conflict, despite continuous Indian pressure, and by early September, the talks had collapsed.[85]

Under Siege

However, the Thimpu talks had far-reaching military effects in the Jaffna Peninsula. On 18 June 1985, both the government and the insurgents had announced a cease-fire. It was repeatedly violated during the following months and in turn, these violations were one of the main reasons for the collapse of negotiations. Nevertheless, National Security Minister Lalith Athulathmudai had ordered security forces garrisoned in the northern and eastern provinces to stay in their camps and to cease patrolling operations. All of a sudden, this several months-long confinement changed the nature of the war itself in the Jaffna Peninsula, the very heart of the Tamil insurgency. Undisturbed, the insurgents took the opportunity to further mine all the critical roads in the area. They also surrounded the army camps with fighting positions and bunkers, virtually besieging them. The main base in Palali for example was surrounded not only by bunkers, but also by minefields and fences. The guerrillas often connected their watch posts and fighting positions with trench lines. Hence, from early 1986 on, army patrols systematically met with heavy resistance when trying to venture out of their bases. Furthermore, once the hostilities resumed, camps were almost every night on the receiving end of mortar fire. Besides, several of these camps were small-sized and not surrounded by a significant buffer-zone. Accordingly, soldiers were vulnerable to insurgent snipers.[86] Thus, in the end of 1985, a SLA Brigadier commented that:

> We can never win this war. Our writ does not run beyond the sand-bags that cover our camps, and we can only do holding operations.[87]

Next, the insurgents renewed large-scale assaults against army camps. The Thondamannaru camp was attacked for two hours on 30 October 1985. In the Wanni, the Killinochchi camp was attacked twice by the LTTE in February and June 1986. Both attempts were repulsed with the help of intensive strikes flown by the SLAF, which had deployed its SF-260TP in combat for the first time during the February battle. If such outright attempts to overwhelm a camp remained rare, most of these were regularly subjected to harassment. In the Jaffna Peninsula, and while they constantly kept all the security force's facilities under observation, the Tigers shifted their attentions from one camp to the other, launching limited infiltrations or probing attacks just to keep the pressure on. They also learned to increase the efficiency of their mortar attacks, first by improving their home-made mortars but also by using them in coordination with Forward Artillery Observers.

Hence, by the end of 1985, the SLA began to launch the first of a long series of limited operations to expend the perimeter of several of its camps, usually suffering severe casualties in the process. Security zones, in effect free fire zones, surrounding the camps were also established to deter enemy infiltrations. Furthermore, the army began to launch so-called 'limited operations', the main objective of which was simply to inflict losses upon the insurgents. The normal pattern was for the garrisons to exit their bases and assault siege positions, advancing from one to two kilometres before withdrawing back to their bases. One of the first such operations took place on 23 January 1986, when troops sallying from the Palali base, and supported by APCs, almost immediately ran into dozens of fighters rushed in by the LTTE, TELO and EPRLF, triggering a fierce battle, before withdrawal. At the time, these limited operations were presented as successful in landing heavy blows upon the insurgents but, in the end, it can be argued that they were playing into the enemy hands.

The LTTE in particular was quick was learn how to shape future battlefields to its advantage – instead of trying to confront the SLA frontally. All of the avenues of approach were heavily mined, thus inflicting casualties on the army without taking any risks. Furthermore, the Tigers deliberately left obvious gaps in their minefields to lure the soldiers into killing zones well covered by interlocking firing positions and where they had zeroed in their mortars. In the meantime, militants were much less exposed to army support weapon fire because they

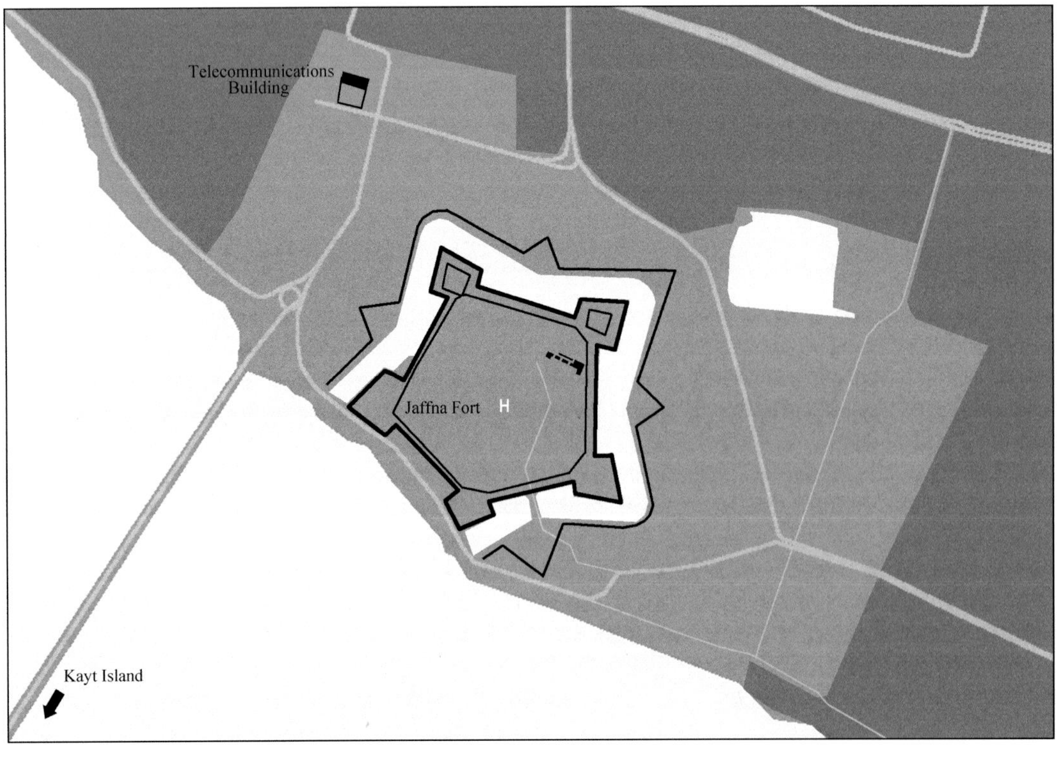

Map of the (Dutch-constructed) Jaffna Fort, with surrounding area. Although an ancient fortification surrounded by the densely build-up quarters of Jaffna (marked in dark grey), and de-facto besieged by insurgents since 1984, the fort remained an important piece of real estate throughout the war. This map shows the position of the Telecommunication Building, north of the fort, and its importance for securing the causeway connecting the fort with the Kayt Island. (Map by Tom Cooper)

One of the primary aims of various limited offensive operations of the SLA in 1985 was the expansion of perimeters around different bases, in order to ease their re-supply from the air. HS.748s of the SLAF played a crucial role in maintaining a constant air bridge to Palali AB, outside Jaffna, and providing 'beans, bullets and gas' to the troops de-facto besieged there. (Albert Grandolini Collection)

LTTE militant armed with a Bazooka; seen while firing on the SLA-controlled Jaffna Fort. (Adrien Fontanellaz Collection)

fought from carefully prepared positions. The net result was that while engaging only a minimal number of its own fighters, the LTTE routinely managed to inflict much heavier casualties on the army than they suffered, thus turning the Security Forces' attrition strategy on its head.[88]

Short Shrift and Giant Step

In May 1986, the SLA came to the decision to launch a large-scale offensive with the aim of re-establishing all road connections to the Jaffna Peninsula. Commanded by Brigadier-General H. F. Rupasinghe, the commander of the Jaffna Security Forces, the operation 'Short Shift 1' was initiated on 18 May 1986 by elements of the 1st and 4th SLSR, the 1st and 3rd GR, and the 3rd (V) GW, supported by most of the 4th SLAR. Three columns advanced simultaneously from the Palali and Velvittiturai garrisons, and from the Karainagar Naval Base, converging on Jaffna. Simultaneously, the troops from the Jaffna Fort – supported by a troop of the SLAC – sallied to take on the insurgent positions around their stronghold.

The advance of three columns was almost immediately stopped by a combination of mines, ambushes, and bridges dropped by the insurgents. At most, the troops advanced a few kilometres. Meanwhile, the Jaffna Fort Detachment faced extremely fierce resistance, and was forced to call off its effort after only two hours. Unsurprisingly, on 20 May Rupasinghe called off this ambitious operation: the perimeters of bases in Palali, Velvittiturai and Karainagar had been expanded, but the insurgents were still controlling all the roads and most of the Jaffna Peninsula.

On 22 May 1986, the SLA launched Operation 'Short Shrift 2', attempting to secure communications with the Jaffna Fort. The latter garrison depended on heliborne re-supply, but this became extremely dangerous because all of the landing zones were within range of insurgent machine guns. This operation was opened by an amphibious landing on the Mandaitivu Island, and the elimination of several firing positions that blocked the two-kilometre long causeway linking the same with the SLA-controlled enclave in Jaffna. Much more successful than the first attempt, Operation Short Shift 2 benefitted from excellent fire-support provided by the SLAF's Bell 212s and SF.260TPs, but also by the fast gun boats of the SLN.[89]

In early 1987, both sides resumed large-scale operations in the Jaffna Peninsula, which remained the epicentre of the war. The SLA simultaneously launched several forays on 8 January, while on 7 February it opened a two-week, coordinated cordon and search offensive, code-named 'Giant Step', in all of the northern and eastern provinces, involving about 5,000 troops in total. This time, the plot was to force insurgents active in the Wanni and the east to withdraw towards the Jaffna Peninsula, while widening the defence perimeter of the 1st GW. In the Wanni, the 3rd SLLI and the 3rd GW advanced from Killinochchi and Elephant Pass towards the Paranthan area, while the 1st GW and the 1st SLLI conducted similar operations in the Trincomalee District. At the same time, elements of the 1st GR had assaulted out of the Jaffna Fort, seized neighbouring buildings, and recaptured the Telecommunications Building.

Although well-planned and executed, the Giant Step failed to have lasting effects upon the LTTE. On the contrary, the militants initiated a counter-offensive: starting in the first hours of 23 March 1987, they distracted the SLA by several diversionary attacks on the Mandaitivu and Kayts Islands, while their main force assaulted the army enclave in Jaffna. A group of Tigers wearing army uniforms managed to infiltrate the Building of Telecommunications – a construction that dominated the causeway linking Jaffna and Mandaitivu. Amid the ensuing chaos, the troops from the Jaffna Fort counter-attacked and cleared the building but, by then, the militants withdrew taking away five army troops and two police officers they had captured earlier.[90]

On 2 April 1987, the LTTE launched an attack on the army base located about 500 metres outside Velvittiturai. Defended by one company of the 1st GR and 25 police officers, this sprawling complex of almost 140,000 square metres was positioned on the coastal road linking Velvittiturai with the Palali base. The attack began around 2300 hrs local time with a combination of mortar shelling and sniper fire. This provided cover for insurgent sappers that cleared a path through the minefield with Bangalore torpedoes. Next, the militants infiltrated the camp and attempted to split it into two: however, the 1st GR had

View of the eastern side of the Jaffna Fort. Although centuries-old, this was still an imposing military position in 1987. (Photo by Adrien Fontanellaz)

Southern gate of the Jaffna Fort, as seen in 2017. (Photo by Adrien Fontanellaz)

A still from a video taken from the Jaffna Fort, showing one of many barricades erected by the insurgents in the streets surrounding the ancient fortification in 1986. (Adrien Fontanellaz Collection)

requested – and received – artillery support from batteries located in neighbouring bases. Well-coordinated fire by the latter forced the surviving LTTE to withdraw, leaving behind 15 KIA, and their arms.

During this operation, the insurgents came very close to shooting down a SLAF helicopter. Soon after the start of the attack, two Bell 212 gunships took off from Palali and strafed areas designated by besieged soldiers. The helicopters reloaded their ammunition and refuelled, and then returned for the next attack. Soon after the dawn of 3 April, the crew of the Bell 212 with serial CH-537 then sighted an LTTE vehicle carrying a 12.7mm machine gun. The gunship engaged with its gun pods while underway at a very low altitude, but the insurgents returned fire from another, previously undiscovered, position. The pilot pulled up to evade, but his helicopter was hit by a burst of 12.7mm rounds: the badly damaged Bell 212 barely managed it back to Palali.

The LTTE launched its next assault on 22 April 1987, this time targeting a detachment of the 4th SLSR that protected the port of Kankeesanhurai. Using a truck covered with sandbags, the militants breached the position and killed 16 troops before being forced to withdraw by reinforcements from neighbouring units rushed from Velvittiturai.[91]

Air War

By the mid-1980s, airpower began playing a crucial role in the war, foremost due to the increased capabilities of the SLAF – not only in terms of fire-power, but because of the availability of bigger transport aircraft and their supply flights to Jaffna. Unsurprisingly, the insurgents began searching for the ways to shoot down some of these. Indeed, when the LTTE received its first shipment of RPG-7s, it opted to deploy these precisely for such tasks. On 23 January 1985, militants hiding near the Palali AB fired an RPG-7 at a DC-3 that was rolling for take-off. The rocket did score a hit, but failed to detonate, and the crew returned for a safe landing at the same base.

By early 1986, the LTTE introduced its first 12.7mm HMGs mounted on pick-up trucks, and used as a sort of 'self-propelled anti-aircraft artillery'. They remained the most potent anti-aircraft weapons in the hands of the Tigers for years. Their appearance forced the SLAF pilots to fly higher, with 3,000 feet (914m) being the lowest altitude considered as 'safe' – because that was the limit of the range for 12.7mm weapons. Luckily for the SLAF, such machine guns remained few in numbers. Combined with the huge area in which they were deployed, the chances of them actually getting into a position to shoot

Although not perfectly satisfying the SLAF's needs, the Bell 212 became the mainstay of its helicopter fleet: no less than 22 were acquired between 1983 and 1987. They served for troop-transport, but also as gunships armed with gun-pods and unguided rockets. (SLAF)

Heavy machine guns – like this Browning M2, 12.7mm calibre – were a relatively rare appearance in the arsenal of Tamil insurgents, and thus considered precious. Most were mounted on 4WD technicals and deployed as 'self-propelled anti-aircraft artillery', with at least some success. (Rohan Gunaratna)

RPG-7s became available to the Tamil insurgents on Sri Lanka in early 1985, and provided the militants with their first 'stand-off' weapon. (Albert Grandolini Collection)

down an aircraft or a helicopter remained slim. Nevertheless, the LTTE continuously and carefully monitored aerial operations around Jaffna, and began developing appropriate air defences. Observers around Palali sounded sirens as soon as they noticed an aircraft rolling for take-off, providing one, sometimes two minutes advance warning. Next, the militants began monitoring ingress and egress routes used by helicopters, and attempted to set up ambushes for these by positioning heavy machine guns right underneath. Several times, they attempted to coordinate machine-gun-fire with mortars. In another case, they attempted to blow-up a helicopter in-flight by detonating a massive land mine buried underneath its flight route. Such efforts were one of the primary reasons for the SLA's attempts to expand the perimeters around its bases in 1986.

At least according to official Sri Lankan sources, all the insurgent efforts remained fruitless, despite few 'close calls'. For example, on 18 December 1986, a Bell 412 with serial CH-523 was flying several passengers from Vavuniya to Mannar. While underway, the crew sighted a civilian truck underway on a secondary road. The SLAF pilots were aggressive, and trained to engage any 'targets of opportunity'. Correspondingly, the crew swiftly changed course and descended in order to attack. As the Bell approached, the insurgents in the vehicle opened fire with their machine gun. The gunner on the helicopter's door followed the suit, forcing the vehicle to stop, and its occupants to scatter underneath nearby trees. Hours later, on its return flight from Mannar to Vavuniya, the crew of the CH-523 sighted the same truck again, and this time decided to finish off the vehicle. However, as the helicopter approached, it came under fire from an RPG-7 team hidden nearby. Fortunately for the crew, the militant had forgotten to remove the rocket's safety pin, and his round thus scored a direct hit but failed to detonate: namely, the rocket was deflected when hitting the hand of a passenger and then flew upward where it cut the fuel line feeding the starboard engine, and embedded itself near the port engine. Although left with only one operating engine, Flight Officer G. P. Bulathsinghala and Officer Cadet HMSKP Kotakadeniya safely nursed the helicopter back to Vavuniya.

However, there are strong indications that the SLAF actually did suffer a number of losses during the period 1984-1986. Not only that,even the official sources cite no less than 22 different SLAF aircraft and helicopters as hit by ground fire during the time, but it is also known that numerous helicopters were lost. A Bell 212 with unknown serial was written off under unclear circumstances on 18 May 1984; the Bell 206A CH556 crashed in the Batticaloa lagoon, possibly as a result of sabotage, on 27 May 1984; Bell 206A CH555 crashed at Palali on 30 November 1984; another Bell 206A appears to have been shot down over Jaffna at an unknown date in 1985, and a Bell 212 CH544 was written off under unclear circumstances on 11 October 1986. Personnel losses remained limited, nevertheless – perhaps also because of the deployment of foreign mercenaries. At least three Sri Lankan pilots are known to have been killed in the crashes described above, near Batticaloa and Palali, in 1984, while another pilot and a cadet were killed in a training accident with a SF.260TP. Further 16 SLAF personnel were killed in land ambushes (including seven in a single attack on 18 April 1986).[92]

In turn, the SLAF's SF.260TPs and Bell 212s proved capable of delivering devastating blows upon the insurgents – especially when the latter were caught in the open. For example, on 20 June 1986, a Bell 212 in 'Trooper' configuration was dispatched to support an army outposts near Kankeesanhurai, attacked by a platoon-sized group of militants. The British pilot (contracted via the Keeny Meeny Services), latter recalled:

> From 1500 feet it was so easy to see it all: the black-clad figures of the Tigers as they dashed from one piece of cover to the next along the northern edge of the village. The puffs of smoke as they fired at the soldiers trapped in their outpost … I put the Trooper into a steady right-hand orbit at 1500 feet over the village…First this way and then other. From number two gunner to number one

and back again. The gunners reloading whilst on the outside of the turn. Lovely figures of eight, laying down an almost constant stream of 7.62mm covering fire…It was like firing down a funnel with the target in the middle at the bottom. It was almost impossible to miss. The gunners rapidly improved their aim and quickly learned to control their bursts of fire to 15 to 20 rounds at time. Roshan [the pilot, author's note] improved his flying and for a brief time overcame his fear. The Tigers were shooting back by then, but the soldiers at the roadblock had actually got their heads up above the parapet and were starting to withdraw to their camp at Tondamanna, 800 metres away, laying down their own covering fire as they went.

The Tigers were getting it from both sides now, and they decided to head for cover. That was a bad move, as we could see behind walls from up there and 7.62mm bullets go through corrugated tin and asbestos roof with ease. Black-clad figures, looking like matchstick men from 500 yards up, dashed between the bougainvillea bushes and the jacaranda trees. They ran from bush to wall to tree in an effort to save themselves from the withering hail of fire. Some didn't make it. On the way they seemed to trip over the odd root or branch from the tree of life and lie still, huddled figurines sprawled in death on the ground.

We put four boxes of ammo down on those Tigers that afternoon, about 1000 rounds, before the Army had successfully completed their withdrawal to Tondamanna with no further casualties…To give them their due, those Tigers at Tondamanna sent a few back at us, but somehow the fact that we could see them for a change and were laying it down on them made all the difference.[93]

Starting in 1984, the LTTE began constructing numerous small camps in the jungle of the Eastern Province. Although their numbers were still small, their armament was slowly improving, and their presence paralysed much of the public life. (Albert Grandolini Collection)

The typical countryside in the Killinochchi area offered at least as many opportunities for ambushes as most of the countryside in northern Sri Lanka. (Photo by Adrien Fontanellaz)

Wanni and the East

If the war in the Jaffna Peninsula had turned relatively static by 1987, operations remained much more fluid in the two other main theatres, the Wanni and the Eastern Province, where the conflict remained in essence much more akin to a classic guerrilla conflict. In the Wanni, the insurgents were not strong enough to besiege the army garrisons and conducted hit and run attacks from a number of bases and camps hidden in the jungles which covered large parts of the area. In particular, they often targeted road traffic along the A9 road, and continued to use landmines to inflict heavy casualties to the army forces. In turn, the latter conducted countless patrols and cordon and search operations, such as in November 1986, when the army claimed to have killed 12 insurgents during a large-scale search operation in the Mullaitivu jungles. Still, these failed to prevent the situation worsening, noticeably because there were by far not enough troops to permanently cover the ground and keep the militants on the run. The Security Forces also lacked any mobile force which could have been swiftly deployed from one point to another to hunt for groups of insurgents just after an attack. While the militants avoided head-on engagements with the army most of the time, there were nonetheless several fierce encounters.

Namely, in October 1986, the SLA launched a large-scale operation in the Mannar district, intending to search and clear the Adampan area where several LTTE camps were located. Brigadier Denzel Kobbekaduwa, in charge of the operation, used two separate forces. The first advanced from the southwest and was acting as bait, while the second force advanced from the northwest to corner the insurgents. Victor, the LTTE's Mannar area commander, decided to mobilise his fighters – including the movement's first female units, which had been placed under his command and had not gained combat experience yet – and to defend Adampan town head on. On 23 October 1986, a fierce and hours-long firefight occurred between the soldiers and the insurgents. At the end of it, at least 20 insurgents, including several female fighters and Victor himself, had been killed, as well as 16 soldiers. The Tigers remained in control of the town and had taken two POWs, as well as nine dead soldiers' bodies, which were sent to Jaffna and exposed for propaganda purpose.

The situation was even more complex in the Eastern Province, composed of the Trincomalee, Batticaloa and Ampara districts, because the population was ethnically mixed – with around 21% Sinhalese, 40% Tamils and 37% Muslims (in comparison, the vast majority of the population in the Wanni and the Jaffna Peninsula were Tamils). Hence, it is mostly in the east that the LTTE conducted its attacks against Sinhalese settlers, often in retaliation for security forces' offensives both in the east, or in other regions, and also to disrupt the Minister of National Security Grand Strategy. From 1984 on, the insurgents established bases in the numerous jungles of the province and progressively increased their activities. As a result, if the Security Forces remained in control of the towns and the main roads, insurgents took control of large parts of the countryside.

Correspondingly, the security forces conducted large scale cordon and search operations on several occasions, but with the usual limited results. At best, they disrupted insurgents activities, inflicted casualties, and even occupied and destroyed some of their base camps – as exemplified by the Operation Ranthambili (Golden King Coconut), launched in mid-1986. In the course of that enterprise, the SLA in the Trincomalee district took a large insurgent camp at Nilaveli, which was protected by a network of trenches and bunkers connected by field telephones. It claimed to have killed 33 militants and arrested 97 others. However, even this success left no lasting impression upon

A still from a video showing a pair of TELO militants armed with MG-34 light machine gun of German origin. (Adrien Fontanellaz Collection)

The LTTE leader posing in camouflage fatigues of British origin in 1986. ((Adrien Fontanellaz Collection))

A still from a video showing a TELO militant with an AKM or AK-47 assault rifle in 1986. (Adrien Fontanellaz Collection)

With the LTTE taking over whatever was left of the PLOTE and the TELO, the group was in a position to start training new recruits inside Sri Lanka too. Here a scene from one of the training camps of the mid-1980s. (Albert Grandolini Collection)

the insurgents, or affected their ability to reorganise and reoccupy lost positions. Before long they returned to the area and continued harassing security forces and Sinhalese settlements.

Altogether, the war continued to become increasingly deadly for the fighters from both sides. Through the year 1986, the SLA suffered 192 and the LTTE 258 KIA.[94]

The End of the TELO

The year 1986 was a turning point in this conflict also because the LTTE gained supremacy over all other Tamil insurgent groups. Although several of the 'big five' were routinely cooperating while fighting the security forces, their mutual relations were plagued by continuous disagreement. By April 1986, the TELO was decisively weakened by internal rifts which ended with the assassination of Das, and the subsequent desertion of its best fighters. The LTTE almost immediately seized the opportunity: exploiting its superior organisational abilities and a better communications network, it concentrated a large number of well-equipped militants in Jaffna, pretexting an imminent large-scale operation against an army camp. The TELO completely failed to identify the threat and thus was wholly unprepared for what was to happen after the next mutual disagreement. When the TELO militants arrested two Tigers and later executed another who attempted to negotiate, it provided the casus belli to the LTTE. At 1100 hrs on 29 April 1986, the Tigers unleashed their killing blow. They simultaneously attacked 24 TELO camps in the Jaffna Peninsula, including their headquarters in Kalyankadu. With most of the competing militants busy besieging SLA garrisons, their rear bases had next to no defences. Unsurprisingly, most were quickly overrun, and the LTTE killed or captured hundreds in a matter of few hours. Some of the TELO fighters managed to escape and tried to reorganise themselves to resist during the aftermath, but they were mercilessly tracked down. The Tigers made it known in public, than any civilian offering shelter to the defeated militants would face deadly consequences. Next, the LTTE publicly tortured and executed dozens of prisoners, sometimes also burning their bodies after executing them.

The last TELO leader, Sri Sabaratnam, managed to hide for a while, but the Tigers found him in Kuttu, a suburb of Jaffna. He was executed on the spot, on 7 May 1986. In India, TELO trainees in camps in Tamil Nadu tried to rally to Jaffna to engage the LTTE, but their four boats were intercepted by the SLN, and all were imprisoned.

Similar scenes took place in eastern Sri Lanka too. The LTTE launched its attack on 29 April, causing a loss of between 150 and 400 militants to the competing organisation, while another 400 were reportedly captured. The blow proved to be fatal for the TELO: this group never regained even a minor part of its former strength and influence.[95]

A Civil War in a Civil War

Strikingly, the other Tamil insurgent groups all failed to react. Instead, they all continued maintaining – even if perfunctory – military cooperation with the LTTE, as if nothing happened. The PLOTE continued manning its defensive positions around the Jaffna Fort and – together with EROS – even launched a joint attack on the same, together with the LTTE, on 9 September 1986.

However, Pirabhakaran did not forget his enmity to Uma Maheshwaran, and was only waiting for a suitable moment. Indeed, it seems the PLOTE leadership eventually concluded that the situation was hopeless: with only five camps in the Jaffna Peninsula, the movement was much weaker than the TELO, and its chances of successfully facing an onslaught of the Tigers were virtually zero. Correspondingly, on 29 October 1986, the PLOTE withdrew the bulk of its forces from Jaffna and announced that it would suspend its further activities in the area, 'to prevent a bloodbath'. Pirabhakaran wasted no time: the Tigers immediately moved in, took over all the positions and even captured the PLOTE's military commander of Jaffna, then executed him, in December 1986.

EPRLF was the next on Pirabhakaran's 'to do' list. On 14 December, the LTTE suddenly announced the disbandment of that organisation, the PLOTE, and the TEA (the most active and best known insurgent group outside the 'big five'). When these failed to react, the Tigers moved in during the evening of 19 December, launching a coordinated crack-down on all of the EPRLF camps in northern Sri Lanka. Around 100 militants were killed although offering virtually no resistance.

While thus eliminated from the north with a single blow, the EPRLF remained a significant force in the east. This even more so because the EROS – the last autonomous major insurgent group – was meanwhile generally considered an 'LTTE proxy'. By the early part of 1987, the LTTE was thus free to assert control on the civilian population in Jaffna, and accelerate the creation of rural courts and vigilant committees. Far from being universally welcomed by the local population (the Tigers tightened their grip rather gradually, while the population was welcoming them foremost because they restored at least a semblance of law and order), the movement made it clear that engaging in political activities for anybody else was certain to result in drastic prosecution. After suppressing all dissent, the Tigers came into a position to raise taxes from the population of the Jaffna Peninsula and, more importantly, receive all the funding from the Tamil Diaspora abroad.

Thus, although the LTTE's units were forced to take over the positions formerly occupied by militants from other groups, the movement greatly increased its military potential. The Tigers captured all there was of TELO's and EPRLF's arsenals, including the superior mortar technology and related specialists of the latter. The importance of the resulting 'industry' became obvious in February 1987, when Colombo banned the supply of steel, and of any kind of spare parts made of metal, to the Jaffna Peninsula – in a vain attempt to deprive the local workshops of the commodities necessary to continue production of mortars, land mines, and various ammunition.[96]

CHAPTER 8
OPERATION LIBERATION

Through early 1987, the government in Colombo ordered the preparation of an unprecedented, multi-staged offensive with the aim of reasserting control over the Jaffna Peninsula. The resolve of political and military leaders was further strengthened by an LTTE attack on several civilian buses in the Trincomalee District, on 17 April 1987, which left 117 dead; and a car bomb in Colombo, which killed another 110 people, a few days later.

The operation code-named 'Liberation' was very carefully planned by top commanders of the SLA, the SLN, and the SLAF. Its first phase targeted the Vadamarachchi administrative sector – the primary rear base of the LTTE, housing most of its workshops and depots, and separated from the rest of the peninsula by the Vadamarachchi Lagoon. Attacking this area offered several advantages. The local coast was one of militant's primary shipping points; the town of Velvittiturai was the LTTE's birthplace; and this area was the least populated of all of Jaffna, thus offering enough space for the military to challenge and destroy the militants in an open battle.[97]

Correspondingly, the SLA deployed a large concentration of troops at Palali, which was to serve as the point of departure for this offensive's primary thrusts. For this part of Operation Liberation, the SLA established three brigade-sized formations. Most important amongst these were:

- 1st Brigade (also known as the 'Jaffna Brigade'), commanded by Colonel Vijaya Wimalaratne, including the 1st GR and the 1st GW, and
- 3rd Brigade (dubbed the 'Vanni Brigade'), commanded by Brigadier-General Denzil Kobbekaduwa, including the 3rd SLLI and the 3rd GR.

Both formations were supported by one armoured troop (each including two Saracens, one Saladin, and one Ferret), and engineers, while several APCs were used as command vehicles for battalion and brigade headquarters. Furthermore, each was assigned a battery of 120mm mortars and 25-Pounder guns, while additional artillery pieces were positioned in different fire bases around the combat zone.

The – still small – special forces component of the SLA was mobilised for this operation too, while parts of other units were dispersed in different bases of the Jaffna Peninsula and put under the control of the 2nd Brigade, commanded by Brigadier-General Gerry de Silva. All together, these units totalled about 8,000 troops, including about 4,000 assigned to combat units.

The SLAF mobilised virtually all of its flying assets for this operation – a total of about 35 aircraft and helicopters, most of which were forward deployed at Palali AB, mere minutes of flight away from the primary combat zone. Twelve of these – including six SF.260TPs and two Bell 212 Gunships – were assigned the close air support and battlefield interdiction (BAI) tasks, while a further eight Bell 212 were prepared in Trooper configuration. Together with two HS.748s, two Y-12s, and two Doves, they were to serve for transport purposes. Another Y-12 and two Bell 212s were assigned the role of casualty evacuation (CASEVAC), while several Bell 206s and three Cessna 337 were to fly reconnaissance.

The SLN deployed four fast gun boats, including the SLNS

Ranakamee, SLNS *Balawatha*, SLNS *Weeraya* and SLNS *Rakshaka*. Five Dvoras and several other smaller patrol boats were to patrol the coasts and prevent the enemy from escaping to sea. The surveillance and command ships SLNS *Edithara*, SLNS *Abeetha* and SLNS *Wickrema*, as well as the personnel carriers SLNS *Lihiniya* and SLNS *Hansaya* and the landing craft SLNS *Pabbatha*, were also supporting the operation.[98]

Deceiving the Tigers

Because this was the first time for the Sri Lankan military to run an operation of this kind, and then a combined-arms operation too, different services had developed new ways of coordinating their firepower and manoeuvre. Common maps were issued to all commanders: these included numbered circles marking the known enemy positions. This greatly eased the work of forward air controllers (FACs) and forward artillery observers (FAOs), because it became sufficient for these to transmit the circle number corresponding to the target area, and either the artillery, or the SLAF would receive the order to provide fire support. This system was named 'bola' (for 'circle'). The maps in question were re-issued every day, each time with new designations for all the 'circles'. In this way, the insurgents – who were known to have systematically eavesdropped on the military's radio communications – were prevented from reconstructing details of the numbering system, and thus recognizing military's intentions. The system in question proved highly successful, and remained in use over the next decade, too.

Hiding the size of such a military build-up was virtually impossible, and thus the related preparations did not escape the attention of the LTTE. On the contrary, the militants found enough time to concentrate all of their fighters on the Jaffna Peninsula. Therefore, the Sri Lankan armed forces went to great lengths to deceive the insurgent leadership about the area where the offensive would take place. Only a few officers were informed about the plan, while empty SLAF helicopters made numerous decoy flights between Palali and Point Pedro in order to convince the LTTE that the latter would be used as a staging point. Next, during late April 1987, the SLAF – which mustered 1 HS.748, two Y-12s and 1 Heron as makeshift-bombers – flew intensive air strikes on known LTTE positions. These lasted for nearly 20 days, during which different garrisons on the Jaffna Peninsula sallied out of their camps in order to keep the enemy uncertain about what was to follow.

Whether all these efforts were successful in deceiving the LTTE remains unknown. What is certain is that the Tigers concentrated most of their forces in the town of Jaffna and around it. Another large group of militants was deployed to Valikamam to oppose any kind of advance in the direction of Jaffna. This indicates that the LTTE failed to identify Vadamarachchi as the primary target of the imminent onslaught.[99]

Deadly Breakthrough

Operation Liberation was launched in the early hours of 26 May 1987. At dawn, SLAF aircraft dropped leaflets in the Vadamarachchi area, informing the civilian population to rally to specific safe places – such as temples and government facilities. Meanwhile, Bell 212s deployed a party of special forces and the SLN's commandos – about 100 troops in total – near Manalkadu. These two forces established blocking positions to seal the escape routes. Immediately afterwards, the SLAF flew a series of air strikes, which went on for the entire day.

While the Vadamarachchi area was thus put under pressure, other involved units launched their diversionary attacks. Troops of the 2nd Brigade drove from the Elephant Pass, along the Vada Strip and

Infantry of the so-called Jaffna Brigade marching to the starting positions of Operation Liberation. (Albert Grandolini Collection)

towards Sornampattu and Chempionpattu, reaching their objectives without encountering any resistance – and thus sealing another potential escape route. In Jaffna, the troops in the fort, reinforced by commandos, assaulted insurgent entrenchments around them. However, this attack was stopped cold by fierce resistance and the loss of seven soldiers in two hours of action.

The main thrust of Operation Liberation began at 0830 hrs in the morning, when troops of the 1st and 3rd Brigade opened their advance from the Palali complex. Supported by an artillery barrage, the infantry of the 1st Brigade easily forded the Thondamannaru Lagoon in two places. Its vehicles had to wait for the engineers to construct a bridge though. Further west, the 3rd Brigade used an intact causeway to cross the lagoon.

The advance encountered the first resistance as it approached the southern shore of the lagoon, where the LTTE's line around the Palali complex began. However, while receiving relatively little small-arms fire – the Tigers defended this sector with only a small force – the troops ran into an area heavily mined and full of booby traps. This is where the problems began.

Eight engineers were killed by a single mine in the south. Similarly, the infantry platoon on the forefront of the 1st Brigade's advance took 90% casualties within half an hour, while command vehicles of the 1st GR and the 1st Brigade were both destroyed by mines. It took extremely careful work of the engineers and troops to clear at least a few lanes through all of the obstacles and resume the advance during the afternoon. Kamal Gunaratne, then the commander of the C Company, 3rd GR, recalled:

> By afternoon of Day One, hundreds of soldiers were wounded and brought to rear of the battalions. Nobody had expected such a large number of casualties within half a day. Most of the soldiers who were wounded or dead were well trained and experienced soldiers. In some places, they had been subjected to small arms fire but most of the casualties were a result of booby traps and IEDs.[100]

While the 1st Brigade eventually managed to punch through the first LTTE's defence line, albeit at the cost of more than 40 casualties, the 3rd Brigade made an advance of only 500 metres by that evening – and this at the cost of 10 KIA and 21 WIA.[101] Once both units found the ways out of the minefields, the two brigades advanced separately. Colonel Wimalaratne's 1st Brigade continued along the coastal road towards Velvittiturai, and then Point Pedro. Further west, Kobbekaduwa's 3rd Brigade pushed inland along the road to Uduppiddy and Nelliady, in an attempt to envelop the LTTE's bastion in Velvittiturai, before it would turn towards Point Pedro.

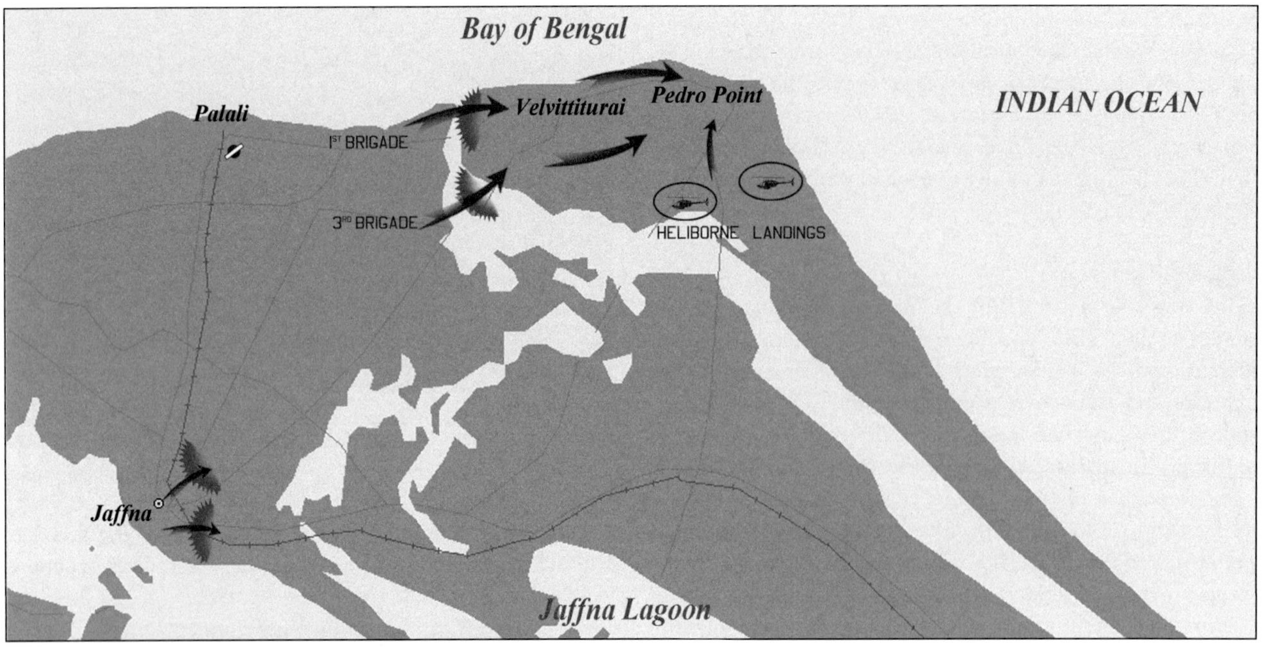

Map of the Vadamarachchi area, showing the primary thrusts of Operation Liberation. (Map by Tom Cooper)

A Buffel of the SLA underway in the Batticaloa area in late 1986. (Adrien Fontanellaz Collection)

While it was expected that the LTTE would launch infiltrations on the flanks of advancing SLA forces, the LTTE reacted with counterattacks on both units. The 1st at least had its eastern flank protected by the coast, but – wary of possible enemy reaction – the 3rd Brigade had to stop time and again to secure towards the north and south. On the other hand, the 1st Brigade had the task of frontally assaulting LTTE's positions protecting Velvittiturai, where Pirabhakaran was suspected to reside since his return to Sri Lanka in January 1987. Although the insurgent resistance was actually no major hindrance, and their losses decreased dramatically once the two brigades passed the minefields, both units were further delayed by bobby-traps left behind by withdrawing militants. One of LTTE's favourite tricks was to wire house-bells or light-switches with powerful bombs. In some streets, one in every five houses was randomly booby-trapped: one such device nearly claimed the life of Brigadier-General Kobbekaduwa, when a soldier next to him activated such a bomb.

Assault on Velvittiturai

The 1st Brigade finally reached the outskirts of Velvittiturai during the afternoon of 27 May 1987, the second day of the campaign. As expected, the defenders – led by the Soosai, the local area commander – relied on numerous strongpoints prepared for months. Some bunkers on the sea-side of the town were strong enough to withstand 37mm shells fired from SLN's fast gun boats, while others were built into apartment houses and perfectly camouflaged. The troops of the 1st GR outflanked these, but did not manage to link up with a detachment of army troops landed by the navy behind the bunkers: this was pinned down by the Tigers, despite fierce fire-support from fast gun boats. Only after being exposed to withering artillery fire and additional air strikes did the LTTE finally withdraw behind a screen of rearguards that began conducing delaying actions. Eventually, Velvittiturai was under the complete control of the SLA by 28 May, and the 1st Brigade then resumed its advance by a push in the direction of Point Pedro.

Following initial problems, the progress in the sector of the 3rd Brigade became swift. Its troops seized Uduppiddy without any major problem. Things changed – dramatically – once they reached Nelliady, where a LTTE party, supported by a technical mounting a heavy machine gun, made excellent use of coconut groves surrounding the town. A series of air strikes by SLAF fighter-bombers and helicopters cleared the area, and finally enabled the 3rd Brigade to invest the town. Even then, further advances remained slow: by 31st of May, this unit seized the Puloli crossroad and could finally turn west to advance in direction of Point Pedro.

Meanwhile, the LTTE in the latter town was already under pressure by the 1st Brigade, and also from within – by the local garrison that made a sally. The militant positions in Point Pedro finally collapsed on 1 June, with which the I Phase of Operation Liberation (also known as 'Vadamarachchi Operation') was closed.

Despite initial problems and heavy losses – the SLA suffered 33 KIA and 182 WIA – the first week of this offensive was an obvious success. The assault came as a shock for the LTTE, the leadership of which failed to identify the enemy 'Schwerpunkt' on time, and thus had its troops exposed to a large-scale, multi-pronged operation for the first time. The SLA claimed to have killed or injured nearly 600 militants, and certainly captured all of their training camps, workshops and depots in the Vadamarachchi area. Over 4,000 male inhabitants were

Typical landscape on the Jaffna Peninsula and much of northern Sri Lanka: open spaces interrupted by thick undergrowth offered endless opportunities for ambushes, but also a good combination of clear fields of fire and cover. (Photo by Adrien Fontanellaz)

The first phase of Operation Liberation saw the SLA's infantry suffering heavy casualties while advancing over extensive minefields protecting the first defence line of the LTTE. Medical units of the Army were soon overburdened by the necessity to evacuate and treat dozens of casualties. (Albert Grandolini Collection)

collected and sent south for screening and interrogation. Certainly, the LTTE was worried enough to launch attempts in the targeted area to recruit former militants of the TELO and EPRLF, including some that were kept prisoners, but such measures came too late. Thus, the only positive experience for the militants was that the bulk of them did manage to extricate themselves from the trap and run away into the jungle.[102]

Correspondingly, on 4 June 1987, the SLA initiated the II Phase of the Operation Liberation. This time the 1st Brigade launched its advance from the Palali complex in the direction of Jaffna town. Its first target was the LTTE's strongpoint in vicinity of Achchuveli. One SLA officer was killed during the assault, but the position fell after a barrage from multiple mortars: around a dozen militants were found inside; including several that had taken cyanide in order to avoid capture. At that point in time, the government in Colombo came under severe pressure from New Delhi, and ordered the SLA to stop the operation.[103]

A crew of a SLA Saladin: as of 1986-1987, such vehicles were deployed in small detachments and used exclusively for providing fire-support to the infantry. (Albert Grandolini Collection)

The First Black Tiger

The setback suffered in Vadamarachchi did not prevent the LTTE from launching attacks on its own. On 2 June, the militants intercepted a bus carrying 31 Buddhist novices in the Amparai District, and summarily executed them – together with four civilians.[104] The next day, the Tigers raided the Telecommunication Building in Jaffna with the help of a truck filled with explosives and protected by improvised armour. The resulting detonation collapsed a part of the building, which then came under assault by several sections – including at least one female unit. The Tigers managed to penetrate the facility and capture a few weapons, as well as three prisoners, but had to withdraw when army reinforcements supported by Bell 212s arrived on the scene. Four men of the 1st SLLI were killed during the attack, and around 40 others wounded. Besides these attacks, the LTTE had resumed the usual pattern of harassment mortar bombing and landmine attacks, while on 30 June 2017, a firefight with insurgents left 12 soldiers killed in action in Kokkilai in the Mullaitivu district.

After the competition of the I Phase of Operation Liberation, the bulk of the SLA troops used in the offensive had withdrawn from the Vadamarachchi area. To prevent the insurgents from reinstating themselves, the army constructed a belt of new fire-bases, in between it ran regular patrols. However, this proved insufficient to prevent the LTTE from infiltrating the area again. Furthermore, by early July the militants introduced a new, devastating weapon to their arsenal.

The 'weapon' in question were carefully selected, highly motivated volunteers, picked to run suicide missions. During a speech to female trainees, in mid-July 1987, Pirabhakaran announced a team of eight 'Black Tigers', who had volunteered to run such missions when and where requested. One of the eight was nobody less than one of Pirabhakaran's own bodyguards.[105]

The first target for one such mission became the new SLA camp established in the Nelliady College. This was usually garrisoned by around 250 troops, mostly drawn from the newly-established 5th GW, reinforced by a troop including one Saladin and two Ferrets from the 1st SLAC, elements of the 4th SLLI, and a detachment of engineers. The LTTE unleashed its carefully prepared assault at the time most of the garrison was patrolling the area around the camp, and only about 100 troops were left to defend the base.

The attack began with a large party of male and female militants infiltrating the camp and taking a position in a row of empty buildings facing the college. They attacked around 2000 hrs, by opening fire at the road-block protecting the main entry to the base. As the troops positioned there took cover, the first Black Tiger suicider launched his attack – as described by one of female Tigers that took part in this operation:

> The army was taken by surprise and chaos broke out. Army men ran from every direction and took up positions near the front of the college. The other women fighters, along with the male cadres in different positions, engaged the troops for 5-10 minutes. We then withdrew some distance from the camp. The firing subsided and Miller drove the vehicle loaded with explosives down the road and through the college gates for about fifty yards. The army was firing at the vehicle without any success. We were lying flat on the ground waiting for the explosion. Suddenly there was a massive blast.
>
> The impact was enormous. Even though we were lying face down on the ground the impact lifted us up and dropped us down again. After the explosion, we all ran into the college to see, if by any chance, Captain Miller had jumped clear. However, all that remained was a huge crater where the lorry had been. The building had collapsed completely. There was debris and dust everywhere. The ground was strewn with dead and injured army men. The army men were shouting and crying. Survivors and some of injured fled to the back of the building. We pursued them taking up positions and firing. They took cover in the back section of the school. A mortar shell from the uninjured troops exploded near us. A helicopter came and started firing. We collected as many weapons and as much ammunition as possible and withdrew. We went back to our camp and celebrated our victory.[106]

Indeed, despite the shock and heavy losses, the surviving troops reorganized themselves and prevented the LTTE from overrunning the college. During the fire-fight, two soldiers of the 1st SLAC attempted to run to their Saladin. However, an insurgent destroyed the vehicle, with an RPG-7 hit killing both of them. Meanwhile, the units patrolling outside were recalled, but their way back ran into several ambushes prepared by the Tigers for such an eventuality. Therefore, the first help came in form of two Bell 212 – one gunship and one trooper – from Palali AB. Their crews established radio contact with an injured radio operator of the 3rd SLLI, around 2300 hrs, and the latter then began acting as a FAC. Thanks to his directions, the fire support provided by just two helicopters became more effective. Eventually, the Tigers were forced to give up their attempt to overrun the camp before withdrawing, and were left without any choice but to run away. Nevertheless, this attack did inflict a heavy blow upon the SLA: not only that 18 troops were KIA and around 30 WIA, but it – as well as another similar assault on an army base in the Vadamarachchi area, on 14 July 1987 – made it clear that the militants were not defeated.[107]

Indian Intervention

Since the failure of the Thimpu talks, India had continued to support the militants as a bargaining tool to leverage the Sri Lankan government into negotiating a compromise. Although President Jayewardene did make some limited overtures, New Delhi was clearly losing its grip on several militant Tamil organisations. Even in Tamil Nadu, the initial popularity of the Sri Lankan Tamil insurgents greatly diminished because, feeling secure in their safe heaven, many broke the local laws. On 1 November 1986, an Indian citizen was killed during an incident in Madras, between EPRLF militants and civilians that opposed them. This incident triggered riots targeting the Sri Lankan Tamil movement, enticing the police to intervene and disarm the militants. Even M.G.R, the so far very supportive Chief Minister of Tamil Nadu, was incensed and made this very clear during a meeting with around twenty leaders of the most important insurgent groups:

'We have given you shelter all these years, but you have misused the freedom. You have begun attacking innocent Indians, It is time all this ended once and for ever and Tamil Nadu is cleared of you all.'[108]

At dawn on 8 November 1986, the police of Tamil Nadu launched the four-hour long 'Operation Disarm'. Simultaneously raiding 30 insurgent camps, it secured and confiscated all of their weapons and ammunition, and arrested several leaders – including Velupillai Pirabhakaran. Things went even more awry on 17 November: during a meeting organized by the Indians where the Indian PM, Rajiv Gandhi, the Sri Lankan President, and several Tamil leaders, Pirabhakaran openly refused to consider any other solution to the Tamil issue on Sri Lanka, but an independent Tamil Eelam. Gandhi reacted by ordering another crackdown against all the militants, this time with an emphasis on the LTTE. However, when Pirabhakaran announced a hunger strike, public opinion turned in his favour – prompting the Chief Minister of Tamil Nadu to return not only all the weapons, but also radio equipment back to the Tigers.

Overall, as of late 1986, there was no solution for the Indian dilemma. At this stage, New Delhi had grown increasingly disillusioned with both the LTTE's uncompromising stance, while forced to acknowledge the movement as the major player among the Tamil militancy, and with the delaying negotiations tactics used by Colombo. Hence, Rajiv Gandhi determined that New Delhi would increase pressure on both warrying parties to reach an agreement that should guarantee the territorial integrity of the island while address Tamil demands for a degree of autonomy.[109]

Jelly Fish and Garland

The major escalation of hostilities in the form of Operation Liberation, and countless reports about large-scale suffering of civilians, had triggered a strong reaction from New Delhi. The Indian government strongly protested in Colombo, but President Jayewardene remained committed to an all-out military offensive. The Indians then upped the ante. On 3 June 1986, a fleet of fishing trawlers operating under the flag of the Indian Red Cross, carrying food and kerosene – as well as journalists – left the port of Rameshwaram, and sailed toward the Jaffna Peninsula to provide relief to the civilian population. Certainly enough, this 'operation' included a military component too. Civilian ships were escorted by the offshore patrol vessel INS *Vikram*. Although operated by the Indian Coast Guards, the 1,200 ton ship was a fairly powerful unit equipped with a 30mm gun and a pair of 12.7mm heavy

Together with the then brand-new Mirage 2000Hs, An-32 transports were the first aircraft of the Indian Air Force to become involved in operations over Sri Lanka – and the sign of what was to follow in the coming years. (Albert Grandolini Collection)

machine guns, and could operate an Alouette III helicopter.

Informed by New Delhi of the approach of the relief flotilla, Colombo ordered the SLN to prevent it from entering in Sri Lankan territorial waters. In turn, the Sri Lankan Navy launched Operation 'Jelly Fish': a task force under Captain Mohan Samarasekera, and including the surveillance and command ship SLNS *Edithara* (which acted as flagship), the fast gunboats SLNS *Ranakamee*, SLNS *Balawatha*, SLNS *Weeraya* and SLNS *Rakshaka*, and the Dvoras P453, P455, P456, P457 and P458, was swiftly organised and set sail to intercept.

Therefore, when the Indian flotilla arrived and dropped anchor at the limit of the Sri Lankan territorial waters, around 1830 hrs, the SLN's task force had taken position and blocked its entry. Following three hours of negotiations, during which Captain Samarasekera had confirmed to its Indian counterpart that he was instructed to protect the national waters 'by any means necessary', the Indians withdrew.[110]

The very same evening, New Delhi decided to launch another operation, code-named 'Poomalai' (Garland). This time transport aircraft of the IAF were to drop air supplies over the Jaffna Peninsula, while in the meantime IAF units in southern India were kept on full alert. At 1500 hrs, the Sri Lankan Ambassador in New Delhi was informed that the Indian planes were to take off one hour later and that any opposition would be met by force. Indeed, at 1555 hrs, the five Antonov An-32s took off from Bangalore airport, while their escort of four Mirage 2000H from No. 7 Battle Axe Squadron departed at the same time from Yelahanka AB. Each of the four Mirage carried three drop tanks and a pair of Magic 2 AAM. The Antonov arrived in the vicinity of Jaffna town one hour later and dropped their cargoes. On their way back, the Indian formation demonstratively overflew Palali: the Sri Lankans made no attempt to interfere and, actually, had no means to do so.

Although the Indian actions were presented as 'humanitarian by nature', and although the Indian violation of Sri Lankan airspace caused a furore within the government and country's armed forces, this sudden escalation of New Delhi's involvement forced President Jayewardene to call off the second phase of Operation Liberation the very same day. Having strengthened its hand, New Delhi resumed its negotiations with Colombo, and extracted a number of major concessions. Meanwhile, it used its influence over the Tamil militant groups to force them to fully commit to the agreement reached between New Delhi and Colombo. Hence, the accord was signed on 29 July 1987. It later included the deployment of an Indian peace-keeping force. Correspondingly, the first Indian troops landed on Sri Lanka on 30 July 1987 – opening another chapter in the 30-year long Sri Lankan War.[111]

Bibliography

Except for sources of reference listed below, the authors made extensive use of the official websites of the Sri Lankan Army, Air Force, Navy and Police, the Indian Coast Guards, as well as the website www.Britannica.com, information mentioned on panels of the Museums of the SLAF, the SLN and the SLA, at the Ratmalana AB (for the former) and Trincomalee (for the latter two).

Amnesty International, *Amnesty International Report*, 1987

Asia Watch Committee, *Cycles of Violence: Human Rights in Sri Lanka Since the Indo-Sri Lanka Agreement*, December 1987

Balasingham, Adele Ann, *The Will to Freedom: An Inside View of Tamil Resistance* (Mitchum: Fairmax Publishing Ltd, 2003). ISBN 1-903679-036

Balasingham, Adele Ann, *Women Fighters of Liberation Tigers*, 1993 online version at tamilnation.co

Balasingham, Anton, *War and Peace: Armed Struggle and Peace Efforts of Liberation Tigers* (Mitcham: Fairmax Publishing, 2004). ISBN 1-903679-05-2

Balasuriya, Mahinda, *The Rise and Fall of the LTTE* (Colombo, Asian Network on Conflict Research, 2011). ISBN 978-955-53071-0-9

Blodgett, Brian, *Sri Lanka's Military: in Search of a Mission 1949-2004* (San Diego: Aventine Press, 2004). ISBN 1-59330-182-0

Boyagoda, Ajith, *A Long Watch: War, Captivity and Return to Sri Lanka* (C.Hurst & Co, 2016). ISBN 978-93-5029-177-1

Chandraprema, C.A., *Gota's War: the Crushing of Tamil Tiger Terrorism in Sri Lanka* (Colombo: Ranjan Wijeratne Foundation, 2012). ISBN 978-955-54087-0-7

Colombage, Jayanath, *Asymmetric Warfare at Sea: The Case of Sri Lanka* (Saarbrücken: Lambert Academic Publishers, 2016). ISBN 978-3-659-86575-6

De Soyza, Niromi, *Tamil Tigress: My Story as a child soldier in Sri Lanka's bloody civil war* (Melbourne: Allen & Unwin, 2011). ISBN 978 1 74237 518 2

Department of Propaganda & Information of Eelam People's Revolutionary Liberation Front, EPRLF, January 1984

Dharmeratnam, Sivaram, *On Tamil Militarism*, via tamilnation.co

DIDR-OFPRA, *Les Tamouls des provinces Nord et Est, fiche thématique*, 3 février 2015

Directorate of Intelligence, *Sri Lanka: The Growing Insurgency*, September 1986

Dissanayake, T.D.S.A., *War or Peace in Sri Lanka* (Colombo : Popular Prakashan, 2005) ISBN 81-7991-199-3

Dixit, J.N., *Assignment Colombo* (Colombo: Vijitha Yapa, 1998). ISBN 81-220-0499-7

Drea, Edward. J., *Japan's Imperial Army: Its Rise and Fall, 1853-1945* (University Press of Kansas, 2009). ISBN 978 0700 616 633

Flintham, Victor, *Air Wars and Aircraft: A Detailed Record of Air Combat, 1945 to the Present* (London, Arms and Armour Press, 1989) ISBN 0-85368-779-X

Fontanellaz, Adrien, 'Guerre au paradis. Le Sri-Lanka en feu', *Air Power Magazine*, No 5, May-June 2017

Goldrick, James, *No Easy Answers, The Development of the Navies of India, Pakistan, Bangladesh and Sri Lanka 1945-1996* (South Godstone: Spantech & Lancer, 1997). ISBN 1-897829027

Gunaratna, Rohan, *International & Regional Security Implications of the Sri Lankan Tamil Insurgency*, (Alumni Association of the Bandaranaike Centre for International Studies Sri Lanka, 1997) ISBN 955-9506-00-5

Gunaratna, Rohan, *War and Peace in Sri Lanka* (Colombo: Institute of Fundamental Studies, 1987). ISBN 955-26-0001-4

Gunaratna, Rohan, *Indian Intervention in Sri Lanka: the Role of India's Intelligence Agencies* (Colombo: South Asian Network on Conflict Research, 1994). ISBN 955-9519-0-5

Gunaratna, Rohan, *Sri Lanka A Lost Revolution: The Inside Story of the JVP* (Kandy: Institute of Fundamental Studies, 2001). ISBN 955-26-004-9

Gunaratne, Kamal, *Road to Nandikadal: True Story of defeating Tamil Tigers* (Colombo: Vijitha Yapa 2016). ISBN 978-955-43237-0-4

Gunaratne, Merril, *Cop in the Crossfire* (Gunaratne, Merril, 2011). ISBN 978-955-53814-0-6

Hashim, A. S. *When Counterinsurgency Wins: Sri Lanka's Defeat of the Tamil Tigers* (Philadelphia: University of Pennsylvania Press, 2013). ISBN 978 0812 244 526

Hole, Rajan et all, *Broken Palmyra: The Tamil Crisis in Sri Lanka, an Inside Account* (on-line version via http://www.uthr.org)

Jeyaraj, D.B.S, '"Great Heroes Day" (Maaveerar Naal) is a LTTE Event and not a Tamil National Day of Mourning', dbsjeyaraj.com, 30 November 2016

Kaarthikeyan, D.R & Raju, *Radhavinod, The Rajiv Gandhi Assassination* (New Dawn Press, 2004). ISBN 1-904910-04-1

Kaur, Minderjeet, 'Warrior Women of old Malaya', *Free Malaysia Today*, 18 June 2016

Library of Congress, Federal Research Division, *Sri Lanka, a Country Study*, 1990

LTTE, *Liberation Tigers and Tamil Eelam Freedom Struggle*, August 1983

Marks, Thomas A., *Maoist People's War in Post-Vietnam Asia* (Bangkok: White Lotus Press, 2007). ISBN 978-974-480-106-7

Mendis, L.M.H, *Assignment Peace in the Name of the Motherland* (Nugegoda: Author Publication, 2009). ISBN 978-955-97640-3-8

Mendis, Nirosha, *The Aerial Tribute: The Role of Air Power in Defeating Terrorism in Sri Lanka* (SLAF, 2014). ISBN 978-9555-0265-19-0

Moore, John E., *Jane's Fighting Ships 1987-88* (Jane's Information Group, 1987). ISBN 978-0710608420

Murari, S., *The Pirabhakaran Saga: The Rise and fall of an Eelam Warrior* (New Delhi, Sage Publications, 2016). ISBN 978-81-321-0701-9

Muttukumaru, Anton, *The Military History of Ceylon: an Outline* (Navrang, Delhi, 1987). ISBN 81-7013-046-8

Narayan Swamy, M.R., *Tigers of Lanka: from Boys to Guerrillas* (Delhi: Vijitha Yapa, 1996). ISBN 81-220-0386-9

Narayan Swamy, M.R, *Inside an Elusive Mind: Pirabhakaran* (Colombo: Vijitha Yapa, 2003). ISBN 955-8095-35-4

Narayan Swamy, M.R, *The Tiger Vanquished: LTTE's Story* (Sage Publication, 2010). ISBN 978-81-321-0459-9

O'Ballance, Edgar, *Cyanide War: the Tamil Insurrection in Sri Lanka 1973-88* (London: Brassey's, 1989). ISBN 0-08-036695-3

Pereira, Gaston C., *Kandy Fights the Portuguese: A Military History of Kandyan Resistance* (Colombo, Vijitha Yapa, 2007). ISBN 979-955-1266-77-6

Pereira, Rienzi, *Wings of Sri Lanka: Sri Lanka Air Force, Fifty Years of Service to the Nation 1951-2001* (SLAF, 2000). ISBN 955-9526-02-5

Pillarisetti Jagan, *Operation Poomalai – The Jaffna Food drop*, bharat-rakshak.com, 5 October 2009

PLOTE, *Our enemy is Imperialism, 1985*

PLOTE, *Batticaloa Jail Break! People's Liberation Organisation of Tamil Eelam's daring Mission!*

Ranatunga, Cyril, *Adventurous Journey from Peace to War: Insurgency to Terrorism* (Colombo: Vijitha Yapa, 2009). ISBN 978-955-665-042-6

Schrikker, A. F., *Dutch and British Colonial Intervention in Sri Lanka c. 1780-1815:* Expansion and Reform, PhD Thesis, 2006

Senaratne, Jagath P., *Sri Lanka Air Force: a Historical Retrospect, Vol II 1985-1997* (Colombo: Sri Lanka Air Force, 1998). ISBN 955-9256-01-7

Senaratne, Jagath P., *Sri Lanka Armoured Corps: 60 Years of History 1955-2015* (SLAC, 2015). ISBN 978-955-1357-01-0

Shamindra, Ferdinando, *An unparalleled daring feat*, The Island

Sharpe, Richard, *Jane's Fighting Ships 1993-94* (Jane's Information Group, 1993). ISBN 978-0710610652

Singh, Harkirat, *Intervention in Sri Lanka: The IPKF Experience retold* (New Delhi, Manohar, 2007). ISBN 81-7304-705-7

Singh, Pushpindar, *The Battle Axes: No. 7 Squadron Indian Air Force, 1942-1992* (New Delhi, The Society for Aerospace Studies, 1993)

Siriweera, W.I & Da Silva, Sanath, *Warfare in Sri Lanka: Military History of the Island from Earliest Time upto Independence* (Colombo: Sarasavi Publisher, 2017). ISBN 978-955-31-0793-0

Smith, Tim, *The Reluctant Mercenary* (Lewes: The Book Guild Ltd, 2002). ISBN 1 85776 6970

Sri Kantha, Sachi, *Kuttimani files*, sangam.org, 5 June 2013

Sri Lanka Army, 50 Years On: 1949-1999 (Colombo, Sri Lanka Army, 1999). ISBN 955-8089-02-8

Subramanian, Nirupama, *Sri Lanka: Voices from a War Zone* (New Delhi: Viking, 2005). ISBN 0-67-005828-9

TELO, *TELO Times*, March 1985, issue no 1

TELO, *TELO Times*, May 1985, issue no 2

Thiedeman, Roger, 'The day the Avro was bombed', *The Sunday Times*, 6 September 1998

Vijasan, 'Lt. Col. Thileepan and Colonel Shankar', eelamview.wordpress.com, 25 September 2011

Wickremesekera, Channa, 'Operation Liberation, 25 Years on', *Groundviews*, 28 May 2012

Wickremesekera, Channa, *The Tamil Separatist War in Sri Lanka* (Routledge India, 2016). ISBN 978 1138 183 117

Wickremesekera, Channa, *A Tough Apprenticeship: Sri Lanka's Military Against the Tamil Militants 1979 - 1987* (self-publication, 2017). ISBN 978-0648134909

Wijesekera, Nalin & Tennekoon, Vijitha, *The History of the Sri Lanka Air Force Vol.1* (SLAF). ISBN 955-9256-00-9

Tamileelam News, July-August 1986 issue

Jain Commission Interim Report, August 1997 via tamilnation.co

'What the British Papers say, Eelam Revolutionaries "Spring Campaign"', *Eelam Studies*, January/June 1985

Notes

1 Siriweera & Da Silva, p.41.

2 More modern interpretations tend to explain the move southward of the Sinhalese kingdoms, and the abandonment of the former capitals of Anudharapara and Polonnaruwa, and their irrigations systems, by the conjunction of several factors adding to the South Indian invasion, such as climatic changes, see Schrikker, pp.15-16.

3 Siriweera & Da Silva, p.42.

4 Schrikker, pp.15-18, Siriweera & Da Silva, pp.27-42 & www.britannica.com/place/Sri-Lanka (extracted 30 May 2017).

5 Schrikker, p.21, Siriweera & Da Silva, pp.81-82, Muttukumaru, p.100.

6 Schrikker, p.26, Siriweera & Da Silva, pp.81-82, 98-102, 109-114, Pereira G., pp.21-32, 64. 94-99, 116-123, Muttukumaru, p.83.

7 'King Rajasinhe' stood literally for 'King Lion', see Anton Muttukumaru, 1987, p.66.

8 Siriweera & Da Silva, pp.47-78, Pereira G., pp.157-162, Muttukumaru, pp.66, 73.

9 Dharmeratnam Sivaram, On Tamil Militarism, tamilnation.co & Drea, pp.119-120.

10 Wickremesekera 2016, p.8, Sri Lanka: A country study, pp.29-32, Hashim, pp.63-64

11 Chandraprema 2012, pp.22-23, 27, Hashim, pp.57-61, 67-68, Narayan Swamy 1996, pp.6-8, Sri Lanka: A country study, pp.31-35.

12 Sirimavo Bandaranaike had already been PM between 1960 and 1965.

13 Chandraprema 2012, p.23, Narayan Swamy 1996, pp.6-20, O'Ballance, pp.2-12, Hashim, pp.68-72, 77.

14 Muttukumaru, pp.113-122, Sri Lankan Army 1999, pp.6-8, Blodgett, pp.21-23.

15 The establishment of the Gemunu Watch did not correspond to an expansion of the army, but was actually a measure of compensating for the disbandment of two territorial volunteer regiments that had only one volunteer battalion each (the 1st (V) Rajarata Regiment and the 1st (V) Ruhunu Regiment).

16 Blodgett, pp.25-27, 35, 37, 49-54, Ranatunga, pp.7-9, 14-15, Muttukumaru, pp.143-150, 162-167, 172-173, Sri Lanka Army 1999, pp.195, 629-643, 664, 904-907, Army.lk extracted 20 June 2017.

17 Senaratne 2015, pp.52, 278, Hashim, p.74, Army.lk extracted 15 June 2017, Blodgett, pp.50-54, Muttukumaru, pp.181-185, Sri Lanka Army 1999, pp.904-907.

18 Blodgett, pp.44-46, 58-61, 79-80, Goldrick, pp.172-179, navy.lk extracted 17 June 2017.

19 The acquisition of the Doves was rather accidental by nature. The RCyAF originally placed an order for six de Havilland Vampire fighters, and these were delivered - per ship, disassembled and packed in crates. However, by the time of their arrival, the Ceylonese changed their minds, concluding that the acquisition of fighter jets was premature. De Havilland flatly refused to return the up-front payment for Vampires, thus leaving the Ceylonese without solution but to buy other aircraft from the same company. Thus, the RCyAF opted for Doves.

20 Senaratne 1998, pp.32-34, Wijesekera & Tennekoon, pp.11-16, 24-46, Pereira, R. pp.15, 20, 23-24, 28, airforce.lk extracted 12 June 2017.

21 Curiously, official SLAF documentation differs in this regards. For example, MiG-17s are described as decommissioned in 1979, 1980, and even 1981 only. It's certain that none were flown after 1979.

22 SLAF history, vol. II, pp.37-38; Wijesekera & Tennekoon, pp.50-58, 64, Pereira R., pp.36-39, 46-54, 60-62, Fontanellaz 2017, airforce.lk extracted 12 June 2017.

23 Sri Lanka Army 1999, pp.62-66, 96, 102, 158, 247, 267, 269, 646.

24 Gunaratna 2001, pp.2-9, 86-89, 102, Marks, pp.207-213, O'Ballance, p.7, Ranatunga, pp.20-22.

25 Sri Lanka Army 1999, p.214, Ranatunga, pp.21-25, Gunaratna 2001, pp.86-92, 94-97, O'Ballance, pp.7-8, Gunaratne M., p.25.

26 Ranatunga, pp.25-27, Marks, pp.209, 214-215, O'Ballance, pp.8-9, Gunaratna 2001, pp.95, 98, 102.

27 Wijesekera & Tennekoon, pp.46-50, pakistanarmy.gov.pk extracted 19 June 2017.

28 According to Thomas Marks, 18,000 people were detained during the unrests, of whom 12,000 were connected - in one way or the other - to the JVP. The government first communicated a total of 1,200 killed during April 1971, while most common estimates mention between 8,000 and 10,000 dead; see Marks, p.209 & Gunaratna 2001, p.105.

29 O'Ballance, pp.8-9, Ranatunga, pp.30-38, Marks, pp.209, 214, Gunaratna

2001, pp.101-105.

30 Balasuriya, p.33, Narayan Swamy 1996, pp.20-29, Narayan Swamy 2003, pp.25-26, 41-42, Marks, p.219, O'Ballance, p.12, DIDR-OFPRA, pp.9-10.

31 Balasingham Anton, p.25, Narayan Swamy 1996, pp.29, 59-62, 69 Narayan Swamy 2003, pp.19-34, 37-41, O'Ballance, p.13.

32 Subhas Chandra Bose was an Indian nationalist who sided with the Japanese and the Germans during World War II, and raised the Indian National Army (INS) in an attempt to gain independence for his country. Considering Pirabhakaran's fascination for Subhas Chandra Bose, it is striking to notice that the INS included a dedicated female unit (the Rabi of Hanshi Regiment), and used suicide bombers. For details, see Minderjeet Kaur, 'Warrior Women of old Malaya', FreeMalaysiaToday.com, 18 June 2016.

33 Henceforth in this narrative, original names of all militants mentioned will be cited once, followed by their nom de guerre (or iyakka peru in Tamil), which will be used in all subsequent citations. One of reasons for this practice is that precise identities of leading Tamil insurgents are often confusing – partially because some of them had several aliases. A notable example was Charles Lucas Anthony, named Seelan but also Aseer. In other cases, the same nom de guerre was shared by multiple persons. For example, Shankar was shared by Kambarmalai Sattiyanathan (one of earliest LTTE militants, killed in the early 1980s), and by Vaithilingam Sornalingam, a high-ranking cadre killed on 26 September 2001.

34 Ranatunga, p.65, Balasingham Anton, pp.26, 30, 34, O'Ballance, p.13, Gunaratna 1987, p.19, Narayan Swamy 1996, pp.60, 65-67, 70, 95-96, Narayan Swamy 2003, pp.38-42, 46, 50, 53, Narayan Swamy 2010, p.IXXIV.

35 For better understanding of local geography it is important to emphasise that Jaffna and Tamil Nadu are close enough for a speedboat to cross the Palk Straits within one hour. In the early 1970s, youngsters from Jaffna often crossed the strait just to see some movie in an Indian cinema, for example. LTTE's communiqué No. 1 was published on 25 April 1978, and claimed responsibility for 11 assassinations since April 1975.

36 Sources differ, but there should have been between 37 and 42 different active groups at the same point in time. See Marks, p187; Gunaratne, R. 1987, pp23-27 & Balasuriya, p24.

37 Gunaratne R. 1987 p.27; Narayan Swamy 1996, pp 41-42, 60, 70, 76, 78; Narayan Swamy 2003, pp.57-61, 70; Marks, p.220; Balasuriya, p.24; O'Ballance, p.17; Chandraprema 2012, p.97; Jeyaraj 30 November 2016; Vijasan 25 September 2011; EPRLF, January 1984.

38 Balasingham Anton, pp.30-34, Narayan Swamy 1996, pp.34-40, 64 Narayan Swamy 2003, pp.39-40, 47, Dissanayake, pp.35-36, 40, Marks, p.265, Thiedeman Roger, 'The day the Avro was bombed', the Sunday Times, 6 September 1998.

39 Gunaratne K. p.40, Ranatunga pp.61-62, Narayan Swamy 1996, pp.41, 65, Narayan Swamy 2003, pp.50, 58, Marks pp.219-220, SLA 1999 pp.290, 311, Dissanayake pp.37, 40, Balasingham Anton p.33, Senaratne 2015 p.99.

40 Sri Kantha 5 June 2013, Dissanayake pp.40, 47, 53, Narayan Swamy 1996, pp.41, 65, Narayan Swamy 2003, pp.50, 58, Ratanunga pp.66-67, 69, Gunaratna 1987 p.20, Chandraprema 2012 p.97, Sri Lanka Army 1999 pp.346, 677.

41 This claim was never confirmed by the SLA.

42 T.D.S.A Disssanayake, 2005, p.39.

43 Chandraprema, 2012, p.106; O'Ballance, p.18; Marks pp.220-221; Narayan Swamy 1996, pp.34, 43-44, 72, 75-77, 82-85, 95; Narayan Swamy 2003, pp.40, 71-77; LTTE, August 1983, pp.29-32; Balasingham Anton pp.34-37; Ratanunga pp.69; Dissanayake pp.39, 47, 49-53; Sri Lanka Army 1999, p.348.

44 Narayan Swamy 2003, pp.3-9, 77, Sri Lanka Army 1999, p.348, Dissanayake pp.64-65.

45 Among official Sri Lankan sources, 'only' 471 were killed in the course of Black July. For details, see Narayan Swamy 1996 pp.75, 93-95; Narayan Swamy 2003, pp.79-83; Chandraprema 2012, pp.111-113; O'Ballance pp.22-26; Dissanayake pp.75, 82-83, 90; Gunaratna 1994 pp.4-5 & Sri Lanka Army 1999 p.350.

46 That the Indian military did consider such an option is obvious by the fact that several Tamil militants had received training in intelligence gathering, with the specific purpose of easing a possible Indian invasion. For details, see Gunaratna, 1994, pp.XII, 6.

47 O'Ballance p.15, Wickremesekera 2016, p.15, Dixit pp.4, 13-15, 19, 23-24, Dissanayake pp.88-90, Narayan Swamy 2003, pp.83-84, 90, 106, 108, Gunaratna 1994 pp.4-6, 30, 34.

48 Narayan Swamy 1996, p.96.

49 Ibid, p.101.

50 Ibid, p.110.

51 Jain Commission Interim Report, Narayan Swamy 1996 pp.102, 108-112, Narayan Swamy 2003 pp.90, 93, 98-99, Gunaratna 1994 p.48, Wickremesekera 2016 pp.15-16, Chandraprema 2012 p.120, Hole, Rajan et al.

52 O'Ballance p.39, Narayan Swamy 1996 pp.120, 130-131, 175, Chandraprema 2012 pp.124-126, 139, Gunaratne K. pp.58, 69, Wickremesekera 2016 p.17, Sri Lanka Army 1999 p.352, Gunaratna 1987 p.47, Thamileelam News, July-August 1986 issue.

53 Hole, Rajan et all, Narayan Swamy 1996 pp.104, 109, 129, 135-136, Narayan Swamy 2003 pp.90, 94, 117, 133-135, Chandraprema 2012 p.125, TELO Times, no 1, March 1985.

54 Narayan Swamy 1996 pp.140, 147, Chandraprema 2012 p.128, Gunaratne K. pp.71, 73, TELO Times, March 1985, issue no 1, TELO Times, May 1985, issue no 2, Sri Lanka Army 1999 pp.677-679.

55 Eelam Studies, 'What the British Papers say', Eelam Revolutionaries "Spring Campaign", January/June 1985.

56 Asia Watch Committee, p.39, Narayan Swamy 2003 pp.90, 119, 132, 150 Narayan Swamy 1996, pp.133-134, 102, 104, 126, 133, 146, O'Ballance, pp.42, 65, Chandraprema 2012 p.135, Eelam Studies January/June 1985.

57 The EPRLF also claimed to have organised this operation.

58 Narayan Swamy 1996, pp.100-105, 112-113, 119, 143-144, 178-179, 186, Narayan Swamy 2003, p.133, PLOTE 1985, PLOTE, 'Batticaloa Jail Break! People's Liberation Organisation of Tamil Eelam's Daring Mission', Thamileelam News, July-August 1986 issue.

59 Narayan Swamy, 1996, p.106.

60 Ibid, pp.100-106, 123-124, 146-147, 171, 209, 222; Chandraprema 2012 pp.120, 132; Hole, Rajan et al.

61 Narayan Swamy, 1996, p.94.

62 Kamal Gunaratne, p.11.

63 Adele Ann Balasingham, 'Women Fighters of Liberation Tigers', 1993 (online version at tamilnation.co).

64 Niromi de Soyza, 2011, p.36.

65 Narayan Swamy 1996 pp.102, 109, 186, 212, Narayan Swamy 2003, pp.91-97, 109, 204, Narayan Swamy 2010 p.IXXXI, De Soyza p.36, Murari p.93, Singh p.154, Jain Commission Interim Report 1997.

66 Among the believed early LTTE ships were the Iliana, Sea Horse, Yelicia, Golden Bird, Ali Toshing, Tony Nova, Yahata, Amazon, Nifly and Horizon. Of course, following the tracks of the ships used by the Tigers was exceptionally difficult as everything was made to hide their real ownership.Several of these were renamed, and Iliana is believed to have been re-baptized to Sun Bird. See D.R Kaarihikeyan & Radhavinod Raju, pp.169-170.

67 Narayan Swamy 1996 p.282, Narayan Swamy 2003 pp.95, 106-110, 116-118, 121, 143-144, 147, 201-203, De Soyza pp.18, 172, 182-183, 205, Singh pp.101, 150, 154-155, 158, Jain Commission Interim Report 1997, Balasingham Adele Ann 1993, Balasingham Adele Ann 2003 pp.76-77, 90, 93, Blodgett p.101, Kaarthikeyan & Radhavinod pp.168-170, Smith p.129, Directorate of Intelligence 1986.

68 Narayan Swamy 1996 p.148, Narayan Swamy 2003 p.123, Gunaratne K. pp.59-60, 62, 78, Gunaratna 1987 pp.40-42.

69 This incident is a good example for many contradictory statements about diverse events during this part of the war. Namely, the incident triggered demonstrations by the local population, which protested against the security forces because the latter had opened fire at the church, which they claimed as empty. In turn, the SLA stressed the building was used as a fire-position by the Tigers in the immediate aftermath of the mine detonation. In the following days, Tamil protesters attacked a Buddhist temple in retaliation, but were dispersed by the security forces; see Narayan Swamy, 1996, p.122 & C.A Chandraprema, p.123.

70 Narayan Swamy 1996 pp.122, 130-131, 140-141, 146-147, Narayan Swamy 2003 pp.111-120, Chandraprema 2012 pp.123-124, 130-134, Gunaratne K. pp.62-63, Sri Lanka Army 1999 pp.677-679, Mendis L.M.H p.48.

71 Narayan Swamy 1996 pp.149-150, Sri Lanka Army 1999 pp.677-679, O'Ballance p. 54.

72 Cyril Ranatunga, p.96.

73 The STF's reputation was such that, a few years later, Indian interrogators stationed in Eastern Sri Lanka would threaten captured insurgents that they would hand them over to the STF if they refused to talk. This threat often proved enough to get the desired result. See M.R Narayan Swamy, 2010, p.IXV for details. Gunaratne M. pp.49-51, Gunaratne K. pp.69-70, Narayan Swamy 2010, pp.XXVIII, IXV, Wickremesekera 2016 p.40, Ranatunga pp.87-88, 96, Sri Lanka Army 1999 pp.351, 391, Police.lk extracted 7 August 2017.

74 Narayan Swamy 1996 p.131, Wickremesekera 2016 pp.34, 37, Chandraprema 2012 pp.130, 154-155, Colombage pp.58-62, 181, Goldrick pp.180-181, Blodgett pp.101-104 , Mendis L.M.H pp.42, 44, Boyagoda pp.45, 55, 61, Ranatunga p.88, Sharpe p.608, Moore p.470, navy.lk extracted 10 August 2017, Shamindra extracted 11 August 2017.

75 Tom Smith, pp.93-95.

76 Chandraprema 2012 pp.129-130, Ranatunga p.97, Wijesekera & Tennekoon pp.70, 72-73, Senaratne 1998 pp.16-17, 23, 40, 45-49, 54-63, 66, 71-79, 83-84, 90, Pereira R. pp.67-71, 76, 80, 83-86, Mendis N. pp.22-25; various panels at the SLAF Museum as of May 2017.

77 Sri Lanka Army 1999 pp.310-311, 377, 391, 396, 636-637, Chandraprema 2012 pp.104, 132, 156, Gunaratne K. pp.40-44, 95, Ranatunga pp.88-93, Muttukumaru pp.196, 205, Blodgett p.94, Marks pp.236, 239, Wickremesekera 2016 p.37.

78 Sri Lanka Army 1999 pp.349, 351, 369, 377, 393; Chandraprema 2012 pp.126-127; Gunaratne K. pp.44, 193; Wickremesekera 2016 pp.40-4; Senaratne 2015 pp.20, 53-54, 57, 79, 99, 103-105, 208, 277-278.

79 Gunaratne K. pp.44, 54-58, 67, Marks pp.233-234, Directorate of Intelligence p.11, Narayan Swamy 1996, p.136, Wickremesekera 2016 pp.38-39.

80 Wickremesekera 2016 pp.38-39, Narayan Swamy 1996 pp.148-149, 156, Directorate of Intelligence pp.V, 12, 18, Amnesty International 1987 pp.265-266.

81 Tim Smith, pp.51-52.

82 Ibid, pp.51-52; Narayan Swamy 1996 p.137; Directorate of Intelligence pp.17-18; Wickremesekera 2016 p.43.

83 Gunaratne K. pp 55, 67, 79, 82, Marks p.232. A lengthy and finely-shaded discussion about the armed forces' exactions against civilians can been found in Wickremesekera 2017 pp.85-102.

84 Narayan Swamy 1996, p.150.

85 Ibid, pp.124, 143, 152-153, Narayan Swamy 2003 p.124, Chandraprema 2012 p.136, Dixit pp.28-30.

86 Chandraprema 2012 pp.134, 147, Gunaratne K. p.90, Sri Lanka Army 1999 pp.377, 387, De Soyza p.98.

87 O'Ballance p.52.

88 Gunaratne K. pp.91-93, Narayan Swamy 1996 pp.170-171, O'Ballance pp.56, 58, 64, Chandraprema 2012 p.142. Smith pp.82, 91.

89 Ranatunga p.104, Mendis L.M.H pp.52-54, Sri Lanka Army 1999 p.387, O'Ballance pp.63-64, Wickremesekera Operation Liberation 25 years on, extracted on 22 September 2017.

90 Ranatunga p.98, Mendis L.M.H p.56, Sri Lanka Army 1999 p.396, Narayan Swamy 2003 p.151, Chandraprema 2012 p.158, Wickremesekera, Operation Liberation 25 years on extracted on 22 September 2017.

91 Chandraprema 2012 pp.159-161, Senaratne 1998 p.79.

92 Chandraprema 2012 p.130; Smith pp.50, 60, 78-82, 104, 128, 136; De Soyza p.41; Senaratne 1998 pp.74-75, 247 & Flintham, pp211-212.

93 Tim Smith, pp.80-81.

94 Smith pp.96, 191, 201; Senaratne 1998 p.72; Mendis L.H.M pp.55-56; Narayan Swamy 1996; p.204, Ranatunga p.98; Wickremesekera 2017 p.127; Balasingham Adele 1993; Hole, Rajan et al.

95 Hole, Rajan et all, Chandraprema 2012 p.145, Narayan Swamy 1996 pp.189-195, 198, Narayan Swamy 2003 pp.139, 207.

96 Related activity continued to result in occasional accidents. For example, on 14 February 1987, 16 Tigers and 46 civilians were killed by the explosion of a massive bomb placed inside a water bowser, which went off prematurely – long before it could reach the Navatkuli Army Camp. Hole, Rajan et al; Wickremesekera 2016 p.18; Narayan Swamy 1996 pp- 206-209, 213, 219-222, 225; Narayan Swamy 2003 pp.139, 14 ; Chandraprema 2012 p.156; De Soyza p.56.

97 Wickremesekera 2017 pp.147-149.

98 Wickremesekera 2017 pp.149-152, Senaratne 2015 pp.54, 115-117, Senaratne 1998, pp.79-80 Mendis L.M.H pp.61-62, 81-82, Chandraprema 2012 p.163.

99 Chandraprema 2012, p.164, Wickremesekera 2017, pp.152-153, 176, Balasingham Adele 1993.

100 Gunaratne K. p.101.

101 Chandraprema 2012, p.164 Wickremesekera 2017, pp.155-158, 163, 170 Gunaratne K. pp.99-101 Mendis L.M.H, p.64, Sri Lanka Army 1999 p.686.

102 Chandraprema 2012, pp.164-165, Wickremesekera 2017, pp.160-164, 167, Gunaratne K. pp.101-103, Mendis L.M.H, p.64, 70-71, 77, Narayan Swamy 1996 pp.234-235.

103 Gunaratne K., p.105, Wickremesekera 2017 p.165.

104 Nominally, each male Buddhist has to spend a few months in temps, as a novice, to gain merits.

105 De Souza, pp.121-122; Balasingham Adele 1993; Sri Lanka Army 1999 p.687; Wickremesekera 2017 p.178; Narayan Swamy 1996 pp236-240; Gunaratne K. pp108-109; Chandraprema 2012 pp.167-168.

106 Balasingham Ann, 1993. Miller was the nom de guerre of Vallipuram Vasanthan. It is not certain if he was instructed to blow himself with the truck or supposed to jump out of the vehicle before the detonation – as in the case of the 3 June attack on the Telecommunication Building in Jaffna. It's certain that Milller was posthumously prompted to the rank of a Captain, and afterwards celebrated by the LTTE as its 'First Black Tiger'. Indeed, 5 July became the movements 'Black Tiger Day', on occasion of which commemorations were held in all the movement-controlled areas until the end of the war in 2009.

107 Sri Lanka Army 1999 p.688, Gunaratne K. p.109, Mendis L.M.H. pp.83-84, Chandraprema 2012 pp.168, 179-180, Balasingham Adele 1993.

108 Narayan Swamy 1996, p.215.

109 Ibid, pp212-217; Narayan Swamy 2003; pp.145-148; Dixit pp.58-65.

110 Mendis L.M.H pp.73-75, Dixit pp.96-102 Ranatunga C., p.112.

111 Pillarisetti Jagan, Operation Poomalai – The Jaffna Food drop; Singh, The Battle Axes, p197-198; Dixit pp.102-106; Ranatunga C. pp.112; Narayan Swamy 2003 pp.159-164, Dixit p.84.

Acknowledgments

This project proved possible only because of the significant help provided by a number of individuals to the authors. In particular, we would like to thank Prof. Rohan Gunaratna, Albert Grandolini and Laurent Touchard for providing their aid in photographic, and other forms of research that eventually made this book possible. Last but not least, Jamie Mcintyre from Australia helped immensely in preparation of the colour profiles for aircraft of the Sri Lanka Air Force, and with lists of serial numbers.

All Rohan Gunaratna's pictures come from his own books "War and Peace in Sri Lanka", "Indian Intervention in Sri Lanka: the Role of India's Intelligence Agencies" and "International & Regional Security Implications of the Sri Lankan Tamil Insurgency", as listed in the bibliography.

About the authors

Adrien Fontanellaz

Adrien Fontanellaz, from Switzerland, is a military history researcher and author. He developed a passion for military history at an early age and has progressively narrowed his studies to modern-day conflicts. He is a member of the Scientific Committee of the Pully-based Centre d'histoire et de prospective militaries (Military History and Prospective Centre), and regularly contributes for the Revue Militaire Suisse and various French military history magazines. He is co-founder and a regular contributor to the French military history website *L'autre coté de la colline*, and this is his third title for Helion's '@War' series.

Tom Cooper

Tom Cooper is an Austrian aerial warfare analyst and historian. Following a career in a worldwide transportation business – during which he established a network of contacts in the Middle East and Africa – he moved into narrow-focus analysis and writing on small, little-known air forces and conflicts, about which he has collected extensive archives. This has resulted in specialisation in such Middle Eastern air forces as those of Egypt, Iran, Iraq and Syria, plus various African and Asian air forces. As well as authoring and co-authoring more than 30 books - including an in-depth analysis of major Arab air forces at wars with Israel during the period 1955-1973 - and over 1,000 articles, Cooper is a regular correspondent for multiple specialised defence-related publications.